D1446490

The Secret Sauce for Organizational Success

Communications and Leadership on the Same Page

By

Tom Jurkowsky
Rear Admiral, US Navy, Retired

Air University Press
Maxwell Air Force Base, Alabama

Director, Air University Press
Maj Richard Harrison

Project Editor
Dr. Stephanie Havron Rollins
Maranda Gilmore

Cover Art, Book Design, and Illustrations
Daniel Armstrong

Composition and Prepress Production
Nedra Looney

Air University Press
600 Chennault Circle, Building 1405
Maxwell AFB, AL 36112-6010

https://www.airuniversity.af.edu/
AUPress/
Facebook:
https://www.facebook.com/AirUnivPress
and
Twitter: https://twitter.com/aupress

Library of Congress Cataloging-in-Publication Data

Names: Jurkowsky, Tom, 1947- author. | Air University
(U.S.). Press, issuing body.
Title: The secret sauce for organizational success : communications and leadership on the same page / Tom
Jurkowsky.
Description: Maxwell Air Force Base, Alabama : Air
University Press, [2019]
Includes bibliographical references and index. | Sum-
mary: "This book provides examples of constants that
communicators and their leaders should stay focused
on. Those constants are: (1) responsiveness to the media;
(2) providing access to the media; (3) ensuring good
working relationships with the media; and (4) always
maintaining one's integrity. Each chapter is dedicated to
one or several examples of these concepts"—Provided
by publisher.
Identifiers: LCCN 2019040172 (print) | LCCN
2019040173 (ebook) | ISBN 9781585663019 (paper-
back) | ISBN 9781585663019 (Adobe PDF)
Subjects: LCSH: United States. Navy--Public relations. |
Communication--United States. | Leadership—United
States. | Armed Forces and mass media—United States.
Classification: LCC VG503 .J87 2019 (print) | LCC
VG503 (ebook) | DDC
659.2/935900973—dc23 | SUDOC D 301.26/6:C 73/9
LC record available at https://lccn.loc.gov/2019040172
LC ebook record available at https://lccn.loc.gov
/2019040173

Published by Air University Press in July 2020

AIR UNIVERSITY PRESS

Contents

Foreword

As a professional communicator for over 45 years, I have witnessed tremendous changes in the media industry—most of them driven by technology and social media. However, there are still some constants that communicators and their leaders should remain focused on. Those constants are: (1) being responsive to the media; (2) providing access to the media; (3) ensuring good working relationships with the media; and (4) always maintaining one's integrity.

These constants are indeed the mainstays of a respected and effective communicator. Maintaining them supports the credibility and respect of the communicator and the organization he or she represents. They are also the pillars of being a good leader, regardless of whether that person is a communicator, a line leader, or the chief executive officer in an organization.

In this book, I will provide examples of each of these concepts and outline how important they are to the health of an organization, its leadership, and its communication function. Each chapter is dedicated to one or several examples of these concepts.

Of the four constants discussed, I have been asked on several occasions: "Which one is the most important?" My response is that they are all crucial; however, integrity is the inviolate one. A person's integrity—whether that person is a communicator or a senior leader in an organization—must never be compromised. Once an individual loses his or her integrity, it is virtually impossible to get it back.

It is also important to note the difference between the terms *public affairs* (PA) and *public relations* (PR). Having worked on both sides of the fence—on the government side and the corporate side—I am frequently asked about the difference or whether there *is* a difference between the two. There is, and it is a critical one.

The best description of the difference is found in an online article on the Government Executive website. Dr. Danielle Blumenthal describes the difference this way: "At the end of the day, the key difference between private sector PR and government PA is who is paying the bill and what expectations they are bound by. The private sector PR expert is trying to help their client resuscitate or enhance their image. The government PA expert is trying to help the taxpayer get the information they need and, more broadly, trying to help the government function effectively and efficiently."[1]

Dr. Blumenthal does a great job of stressing that PA supports the taxpayer while PR has a more profound concern regarding image, product enhancement, and the bottom line. That is why the term PR is verboten in the government. Unfortunately, there are those in the government who forget for whom they are working. The following chapters will illustrate the disservice they are doing to those they have sworn to serve—the American citizen and taxpayer.

I will also devote a bit of time to the concept of leadership itself. Specifically, I will look at what makes an individual a good leader. There are good and bad leaders in both the private and public sectors, and one can learn from both. Every leader develops his or her leadership style and techniques by observing how others perform this all-important function in any organization.

The next few chapters will document some of the significant issues I have dealt with in my professional career—in the Navy, at Lockheed Martin, and at the US Mint. I hope that the examples will serve as another attempt to reinforce the necessary ingredients or the "secret sauce" of good communications and leadership practices.

About the Author

Rear Adm Thomas J. Jurkowsky, US Navy, retired, holds a master of science in public relations from American University and a bachelor of science degree in journalism from Boston University. He is a public relations professional with 45 years of experience in the defense, corporate, and government sectors. He served in the Navy for 31 years, beginning his career in 1969 as an enlisted man and retiring as a rear admiral. Jurkowsky was a public affairs specialist and handled crises such as the loss of sailors' lives, ship collisions, and fires; the infamous Tailhook scandal; and numerous unfavorable incidents at the US Naval Academy. He assisted in the production of several Navy-related Hollywood movies such as *Top Gun*. His final position was as the Navy's chief of information, as the Navy's chief spokesman and head of its entire public affairs efforts. After retiring from the Navy in 2000, Jurkowsky served as the vice president for media relations for Lockheed Martin. After retiring from Lockheed, Jurkowsky joined the US Treasury Department, where he served as the US Mint's chief of corporate communications. He serves on the board of the Military Officers Association of America and has served as an adjunct instructor in communications at Anne Arundel Community College in Arnold, Maryland. Jurkowsky is married and lives in Annapolis, Maryland.

Acknowledgments

I am very grateful for the many mentors I have had during my career. I discuss some of them in this work, but the one who convinced me to pursue this project was the gentleman who hired me at the US Mint—Edmund "Ed" Moy. Ed served at the White House before being named by Pres. George W. Bush as the thirty-eighth director of the Mint. Ed was a terrific boss and let me "do my thing." Whenever we would have lunch or a personal discussion, I would frequently recall many of my Navy experiences (I would refer to them as "sea stories"). After listening to them, Ed would always urge me to write a book and recount them.

After much cajoling, he convinced me to undertake this project. Throughout this endeavor, Ed was incredibly supportive, and I am most grateful for his encouragement and friendship. I feel very blessed that Ed came into my life. He is the consummate gentleman.

I must also give a considerable set of Navy BZs (a Navy term for kudos) to retired Cdr Joseph "Joe" Quimby. Joe and I "go way back," as they say, and he has always been a loyal shipmate. In addition to his loyalty, Joe is also brilliant. He was an extraordinary Navy public affairs officer—one of those officers you want with you when the going gets tough and when you require honest input and recommendations. He agreed to be my editor, before turning the reins over to Maranda Gilmore and Dr. Stephanie Rollins at the Air University Press, and I cannot thank Joe enough for his efforts. Joe is tremendous and always found a better word, a better phrase, a better example, or a better way to express something. He was never afraid to throw a "red flag" on me, and for that, I am most thankful.

Another extraordinary "soul mate" is retired Navy Capt Thomas "Tom" Corcoran. Tom and I met and worked together when we were assigned to the staff of Adm Carl Trost, the chief of naval operations from 1986 to 1990. I was the admiral's special assistant for public affairs, and Tom was his speechwriter. Tom is one of the brightest minds I have ever worked with—extremely cerebral, a master of the written word, and a great sounding board. He commanded two ships, which in itself speaks volumes about his capabilities. Commanding one ship is an accomplishment; however, commanding two reflects the respect and confidence the Navy had in him. One of his last jobs was as a military assistant to then-Secretary of Defense Les Aspin—a "plum" job, and one that marked him to be a future admiral himself. Ultimately,

Tom decided to leave the Navy and pursue a writing career of his own. He has been a great supporter of this book, and I appreciate his encouragement and insight—but most of all, his friendship.

I must also thank a wonderful family friend and cheerleader, Patty Suriano. Patty was a big supporter of this project and a huge help with her technology expertise.

As I age and reflect on all of my many mentors, I will always remember my first shipboard commanding officer—Vice Adm J. R. Sanderson. Sanderson was captain of USS *Saratoga*, an aircraft carrier, and my first ship. He taught me leadership in a big way and also how to handle a ship. What an opportunity! I later served with him again when he was a rear admiral as commander of Battle Force Sixth Fleet. He then became a vice admiral (a three-star). I think of him very often.

I am also grateful to Rear Adm John Bradford "Brad" Mooney, a diesel boat submariner who built himself quite a resume because of his skills as a submariner and deep-sea diver. He was the captain (my boss) at the Naval Training Center in Orlando, Florida, when I was a mere lieutenant. He was another mentor who let me "do my thing." That job was one where I started to "cut my teeth" as a public affairs officer.

I have fond memories of Vice Adm Crawford A. "Pete" Easterling. He was commander of the Naval Air Force, US Pacific Fleet. Anything that had to do with naval flight was his domain—six aircraft carriers, six carrier air wings, and air stations west of the Mississippi to Alaska, Japan, the Philippines, and Guam. It was a huge responsibility. I learned so much from him, including his frequent question to his staff when a program, project, or issue arose: "Who's in charge?" That statement has resonated with me ever since. What Easterling was saying was, "Who's accountable for ensuring this project/issue/problem gets resolved? Who is going to see it to its conclusion? Who is going to come to me and tell me I need to get involved?"

Easterling could be rough and gruff, but I loved him. He, too, let me "do my own thing," and this included his fully supporting production of the movie *Top Gun*. Without his support, that movie would have never been made. In all honesty, I think Easterling saw more in me than I saw in myself, and I was fortunate to have him as a mentor.

Another mentor was Adm Carlisle A. H. Trost, whom I served when he was the chief of naval operations. I would always tell people that when you look up the term *gentleman* in the dictionary, there was a picture of Trost. In addition to being a gentleman and a great leader, he was brilliant. When our nation's political leadership selected Trost to lead the Navy from 1986 to 1990, they made the right decision.

I also had the privilege of working for Adm Charles "Chuck" Larson. I discuss my two assignments working for him in-depth in the book. Suffice it to say he was another one of those officers that I can characterize with the following words: gentleman, classy, brilliant.

Rear Adm William "Bill" Thompson, the first public affairs specialist to become a flag officer, was my first boss when I became a designated public affairs officer in 1973. From a public affairs perspective, he took the Navy in an entirely new direction when he assumed his position in 1971. The Navy indeed was the "silent service" when it came to telling its story. Thompson changed that mindset in a big way, and I was fortunate to have served under him.

Moreover, how can I not acknowledge the wonderful men and women I served alongside in the US Navy? We always had a story to tell the American taxpayer and the world because of these people who sacrifice so much each and every day. Unfortunately, the story that my book does not address is the sacrifices that the Navy family makes. The wives and husbands who have to be both mother and father while spouses are deployed for ten months or even a year—frequently in dangerous parts of the world—are the real backbone of the naval service. Nevertheless, they do their jobs, despite not receiving the recognition they deserve.

Lastly, but certainly not least, my wife, Sally, truly deserves top billing. Sally has been so supportive of me and my career. She is talented, with so much to offer; however, she put all that aside to be a *fantastic* Navy wife and mother to two very successful daughters, Sara and Cameron. Sally has made countless sacrifices and never stopped being my best friend, confidante, and advisor. Sally is another supporter of this book. I feel blessed that God somehow felt I was worthy of her.

Notes

(All notes appear in the shortened form. For full details, see the appropriate entry in the bibliography.)

1. Blumenthal, "Difference between Public Affairs and Public Relations."

Chapter 1

The Evolution of Proactive Communications in the Navy
From Vietnam to the Present

My first assignment as a professional Navy public affairs (PA) officer was in 1973 when I was designated to be a Navy spokesman in the Pentagon. I had just returned from shipboard duty aboard the aircraft carrier USS *Saratoga*. We had completed a ten-month deployment to the US Seventh Fleet, where we served as one of six carriers in the Gulf of Tonkin operating off the coast of Vietnam.

During that time in our nation's history, I found it difficult to report to the Pentagon while serving in the military. The Vietnam War was not popular and the mood of the country and its acceptance of those serving in uniform was not like it is today. Those of us returning from service in Vietnam were heckled, cursed, spit at, and even physically assaulted. When I reported to the Pentagon for duty, I was told not to wear our military uniforms to work. The Nixon administration wanted to downplay the military presence in Washington. So regardless of how proud we were about serving our country, we could not show it by wearing our uniforms.

From a leadership and communications standpoint—making matters worse—the media did not trust the military, and the military did not trust the media. The media, after all, were—at least in the minds of some military people—responsible for us losing the war.

After settling into the Pentagon and familiarizing myself with the bureaucracy there, I began to cultivate relationships with the Pentagon press corps. However, this relationship goal soon became very challenging. Whenever the media asked me a question and it required research with the Navy staff, I frequently ran into brick walls. The aftertaste of Vietnam and the media's perceived role in the war's failure led to a disdain for the media on the part of many military personnel. Consequently, it became tough to obtain information or answers to the most basic questions—often taking days to receive information that should have been provided instantly. It was also not uncommon for some Navy staff members to require *any* requests for routine information in writing rather than by the phone or in person. This frequently added significant delays to reporters' most basic requests.

That is certainly not how to nurture relationships with the media or be responsive to their needs.

After the Vietnam War ended, morale in the military became even worse. Since the war was over, Congress cut the Department of Defense (DOD) budget to the bone. Jimmy Carter was elected president, and although he was a Naval Academy graduate, he was also a progressive Democrat who wanted to heal the country from the wounds of Vietnam. Accordingly, we witnessed a rapid degradation of force readiness, and our military was labeled as being "hollow."[1] Diminished funding led to a deficit of spare parts for our ships, aircraft, and land forces; the inability of our ships and troops to get underway to train; and a shortage of money for aviators to fly and maintain their proficiency.

Morale plummeted in tandem with readiness. Unfortunately, this was proven when lives were lost after the US embassy in Tehran was overtaken, and when an attempt was made in 1980 to rescue the hostages who were being held prisoner by Iranian radicals. The rescue mission failed miserably and was an embarrassment for the United States and its military.

Shortly after the indignity of the failed Iranian hostage rescue, Ronald Reagan was elected president, and he promised to restore the military to a battle-ready force with both equipment and people that were ready and trained to fight. For the Navy—among other things—this meant a goal of a 600-ship Navy centered around 15 aircraft carriers; 100 fast-attack submarines; previously mothballed battleships outfitted with new weapons systems, such as Tomahawk cruise missiles; and newly constructed "strategic homeports" on the East and West Coasts and the Gulf of Mexico to ensure political support for the revitalized Navy.

Morale in all the services soared as units began to get the spare parts they needed to train. Reagan also argued for, and won, badly needed pay increases for military personnel. The DOD began with the delivery of new ships, aircraft, tanks, and other equipment. The Navy (along with the other services) was ready to take on the Soviet Union if need be. Restoring battle readiness, morale, and confidence in the military was achieved.

However, that battle-ready "high" was relatively short-lived. In 1989, the Berlin Wall came down, and with it came the end of the Cold War. Two years later, Mikhail Gorbachev, the president of the Soviet Union, resigned on Christmas Day 1991. It really should have not come as a surprise, as just a few days earlier, the entire Soviet Union had collapsed with 11 of the former Soviet republics establishing the Commonwealth of Independent States, effectively dismembering the Union of Soviet Socialist Republics. Realistically, the Soviet Union had already ceased to exist.[2]

The end of the Cold War was an easy excuse to deprioritize US military readiness. The reduced threat trends, along with a deep recession and increased budget deficits, enabled Congress to call for a "peace dividend." Protecting the DOD under the new George H. W. Bush administration became problematic. In early 1989, the administration rejected the DOD proposal of two percent annual real growth and decided on a flat budget for fiscal year (FY) 1990. Although it would not be until 1990 that final budget levels were established, overall force levels and the administration's national security review in 1989 were predicated on the assumption that a 25 percent reduction in force structure and a 10 percent reduction in DOD resources were possible.[3]

With the resultant cuts to service budgets, each service began to look for ways to tell the story of its relevance. Budget cuts were going to be severe, and there was a sudden recognition that we must tell our story—if even just to maintain current force levels. I found it ironic that the Navy warfare branch most adamant about telling its story turned out to be the submariners. Perhaps this was directly related to the success the Navy and its submarine force experienced in the late 1980s while working hand-in-hand with the film production team on the set of *The Hunt for Red October*, which was based on Tom Clancy's book by the same name. Another well-known success for the Navy and the Hollywood film industry was in 1986 with the release of *Top Gun*, starring Tom Cruise and the US Navy.

Previously, the submarine community took great pride in avoiding the media. When I first reported to the Pentagon as a Navy spokesman in 1973, the community's attitude toward the press essentially reflected the attitude of Adm Ernest King, commander in chief of the US Fleet and chief of naval operations during World War II, who said: "Don't tell them [the press] anything. When it's over, tell them who won."

That attitude clearly would not fly today, but the fact that the submarine community turned to the Navy PA community to tell its story spoke volumes. Veteran military journalist Stan Zimmerman captures this turnaround in attitudes after speaking to a senior Navy admiral.

"When I came to Washington, I decided not to talk to the press. In the last two years, I've changed my mind. We've got a story to tell, and I think we ought to tell it."[4]

I used to say—sarcastically—that some individuals would rather get a root canal than have to deal with the media. Nevertheless, as Zimmerman says, "The news media . . . are the conduit for [the] explanation of sea power to the American public and the world at large. Their improved understanding will spread."[5] You can substitute the name of any organization for the words *sea power* because they, too, have a good story to tell.

The submariners were anxious to get media representatives out to our submarine force and observe the professionalism and discipline of their officers and men. The media embarks aboard our submarines proved successful—prompting a desire to do more.

The other warfare communities were also desirous of becoming more open with the media, and the Navy PA community felt like we were on the same team again. There also seemed to be an acknowledgment on the part of the "line" or warfare communities that the public had a right to know what its Navy was doing. An openness began to develop, and we felt we were playing a vital role in the organization.

However, like the cyclical nature of defense budgets that drove service leadership crazy, the attitude about working with the media suffered a setback when Iraq invaded Kuwait in 1990. While some of the other services chose to embed media into deployed units, the Navy took a somewhat reticent approach. I cannot explain why this occurred. However, when the Navy saw the excellent coverage that resulted from the embedded news media with the ground forces, Navy leadership admitted they made a mistake in establishing a more restrictive policy regarding media on board ships in the Persian Gulf.

During this time, I was based in Pearl Harbor at the headquarters of the US Pacific Fleet. Whenever an aircraft carrier battle group commander (a rear admiral) debriefed his battle group's deployment to the Pacific Fleet staff, one of the things that most commanders said was that not putting news media, journalists, producers, and their still and video photographers on our carriers while supporting Persian Gulf operations was a big mistake. Unfortunately, as a result of that policy—of not having the media relay the Navy's story—the critical role our ships and sailors played in the war were never told.

I remember one specific incident of service jealousy that occurred. The Marines played a considerable role in the first Gulf War. One of the decisions by the Marine Corps' leadership was to embed *Washington Post* reporter Molly Moore with selected troops. The resultant stories that appeared in the *Post* were tremendous. For the most part, they were positive and reflected the pride and professionalism of the Marines. Occasionally, Moore would write something negative or that was not entirely accurate. Instead of terminating her assignment and sending her home, the Marine Corps leadership—specifically, Lt Gen Walter Boomer, who later earned his fourth star and became the assistant commandant of the Marine Corps—would tell Moore what she had inaccurately reported or provide additional perspective to a story. Rather than fuming and holding a grudge, the general or one of his staff members would say, "Let's look past this and move on." It was refreshing.

Interestingly, in his first assignment as a Marine Corps brigadier general—well before Saddam Hussein's invasion of Kuwait—Boomer was assigned as the director of Marine Corps Public Affairs. In this position, he was able to gain perspective on how the press worked and its effectiveness in telling an organization's story.[6]

After participating in a panel discussion on the military and the media in 1997, Boomer wrote an opinion column in *Proceedings* and was very pointed in his comments. He stated, "From the military perspective, there is something we need to understand. This is a democracy, and a free press is the fundamental underpinning of everything we stand for, fight for, and believe in. Now, it doesn't make any difference then whether you like the media or you don't like the media—they're here to stay."[7]

Boomer, addressing his comments to the military, went on to say, "Look, figure out a way to deal with this problem [handling the media]. Stop talking about it, stop whining about it, [and] just get down to work . . . . Let us stop talking about this issue and solve it. It's not that big a deal . . . . Both sides need to stop talking about this thing, sit down, and get to work, figure out the few tough issues that we need to work on, and let's learn to live together. Neither of us is going to go away."[8] His comments were spot on, as relevant today as they were in 1997, and applicable to any government agency or corporate entity that has to coexist with the media and is accountable to stakeholders.

Military units, government agencies, and companies frequently harbor fear about providing access to the media. The biggest concern is people internal to the organization. What are sailors, people on the manufacturing floor, or nurses in a hospital going to say about the ship or organization for which they work? Boomer provides a unique perspective to address these concerns:

> If you are going to do that [let the media interact with the sailors on a ship or employees in an organization], you better have faith in your troops. If you don't trust them, you can't turn the media loose. But I would submit that if you don't have faith and don't trust them, you're not a very good leader and you shouldn't be there either. You've got to be able to deal with the one percent that is going to say what you don't want them to say. . . . Ride that storm out; don't shut it down because of the one percent.[9]

When members of the media are provided access to an organization, ground rules must be established. If something is classified or proprietary and cannot be shown or discussed, that should be explained before access is granted. More often than not, all parties involved will abide by ground rules established early in a professional relationship.

The Takeaway

The media's access to an organization can help shape or enhance the opinions of that organization. In General Boomer's case, the Marine Corps already had a solid reputation and "brand" well before Operation Desert Shield. The resultant news stories from the *Washington Post* reinforced that reputation. Access helps establish greater credibility—a news story about an organization says the organization is important and has something to say.

Providing access to the media allows an organization an opportunity to educate an audience. In the Marine Corps case, in Operation Desert Shield, the public saw the pride, professionalism, and sacrifices that Marines made in a wartime environment. Permitting the media access to a manufacturing organization or any other entity can showcase the same type of pride and professionalism.

Access helps generate news stories about an organization and that contributes to building support, both externally and internally. Often overlooked are the benefits access provides internally; for example, media coverage can enhance the morale of employees. Working with media organizations to get out urgent news about your organization or production issues is an excellent example of what I call "going external to reach your internal audience." There could be good or bad news regarding a production line for a corporation or a mishap at sea that would spread more quickly to your employees by alerting the media. Your employees will hear it on the radio, read it in the newspaper, or see the television reports. Equally important, so do their families.

Look for those media opportunities, think them through with proper planning and preparation, and do not forget to set ground rules.

Notes

1. Jones, *A Hollow Army Reappraised: President Carter, Defense Budgets, and the Politics of Military Readiness.*
2. History.com Editors, "Gorbachev resigns."
3. Larson, Orletsky, and Leuschner, *Defense Planning in a Decade of Change,* xiv.
4. Zimmerman, *"The Battle of the Lasting Impression,"* 44–47.
5. Zimmerman, 46. Also see Waddle, *Selling Sea Power.*
6. The Marines also have a long history of cultivating their image, see Venable, *How the Few Became the Proud.*
7. Boomer, "Stop Whining," 2.
8. Boomer, 2.
9. Boomer, 2.

Chapter 2

The Navy's Safety Stand-Down . . .

And the Importance of Leaders Telling the Story and Being Visible

The year 1989 was a tough one for the Navy. We saw an incredible number of accidents—ship collisions, midair aircraft accidents, shipboard fires, the accidental bombing of a civilian campground, and a Navy plane crashing into an apartment complex.[1] Earlier in the year, an explosion within turret two on USS *Iowa* (BB-61) resulted in the deaths of 47 crewmembers.[2] "As of Christmas Day, the Navy in 1989 had recorded 75 major accidents and 104 fatalities for the year, including the *Iowa* turret disaster."[3]

I was a commander at the time, working for Adm Carlisle Trost, the chief of naval operations (CNO). I was his special assistant for PA. On 14 November 1989, Trost had seen enough and felt it was time to take a timeout. Although there was not an apparent pattern to the rash of accidents—some being caused by mechanical failure, some by ignoring procedures, and others by human error—Trost ordered a two-day safety stand-down for the entire Navy. This meant all naval activity was to come to a halt while all units, both ashore and afloat, reviewed safety procedures.

I think the incident that caused Trost to issue his order was when two attack airplanes accidentally dropped live ordnance near campers who were about three miles from a mountain gunnery range in California. One camper was slightly injured with shrapnel wounds as a result of the missed target. It certainly could have been far worse.

When the CNO issued the order to the fleet, Trost was meeting with members of the Joint Chiefs of Staff (JCS) in their Pentagon meeting room called "the tank." The meeting had nothing to do with the Navy's safety issues. It concerned the then Soviet Union and the Strategic Arms Limitation Talks. The meeting began in the early afternoon, and when the Pentagon press corps heard of Trost's stand-down order, they began to beat down my door to speak with him. The afternoon wore on—as did the JCS meeting.

As deadlines loomed, the media became quite anxious and felt strongly about the importance of talking to the head of the Navy who issued the order to stand-down. I could not have agreed more. It is also important to remember the year this occurred—1989. There was still a timed news cycle, and the network evening news shows were very much a "thing." Digital and social media were nonexistent.

Trost finally returned to his office at about 5:15 p.m., and I immediately asked to see him to tell him about the media requests. He was tired after spending the entire afternoon in "the tank," discussing a significant and heady issue—strategic arms. After hearing my pleas to meet with the Pentagon media, he said, "Tom, I just want to go home and get something to eat. I'm exhausted. I've been in that room all afternoon, and this is really the last thing I want to do."

After negotiating with him, I was able to convince Trost that meeting with the Pentagon press corps was important. We did not need much time. Ten or 15 minutes would be sufficient, especially since most of the reporters were on deadline. He agreed: "Okay. You win. Tell 'em we're coming down."

I immediately called the office of the Assistant Secretary of Defense for Public Affairs and informed them about the admiral's decision. I asked that the Pentagon press corps be given advance notice that we would be down in five or 10 minutes. I also informed Rear Adm Brent Baker, the Navy's chief of information.

As we walked from Trost's office on the fourth floor of the Pentagon to the press studio, Trost and I chatted about what was going to happen. I told Trost he should make a short statement about why he ordered the stand-down and then take some questions. The event happened flawlessly. As expected, Trost did exceptionally well and handled the questions effortlessly. By 5:45 p.m., he left for the evening.

The news coverage of the stand-down that evening was fair and straightforward, as was the print coverage the next morning. However, Trost had a scheduled hearing before the Senate Armed Services Committee the next day. Before his testimony began, every member of the committee noted Trost's appearance on the previous evening's newscasts. Without exception, every senator on the committee praised him for his decision and said ordering the stand-down was the right thing to do. The senators complemented Trost's explanation to the media and praised him for being visible. It felt terrific to see my boss acknowledged by the Senate committee members, but I felt even better when we returned to the Pentagon.

Trost was as affable as he was brilliant and always took the time to acknowledge his staff. It is one of the reasons he was so well-liked and respected. So, when I went to his office that afternoon, he pointed his index finger at me and moved it as if to say, "Come here, young man." When I approached him, he said, "Now I don't want you to get a big head, but I'm glad I listened to you. Doing that little event with the press corps last evening was the smartest thing we did." Then he smiled.[4]

The bottom line and lesson learned here is that the leader of any organization, large or small, must be visible and willing to explain essential decisions. It truly helps to add context to a situation. The Pentagon press corps could have very easily done the story without speaking to Trost. They had the entire message that Trost sent to the fleet and could have filed their stories without his statement. However, had one of them said something like "Trost was not able to answer questions" or "The chief of naval operations was not willing to address his directive," that would not have been helpful to a tense and serious issue.

A case for why the American public needs to hear from its government is expressed very well by 13 former White House press secretaries and foreign service and military officials in a CNN opinion piece.[5] In writing the piece, the officials were clearly being critical of the Trump administration for the paucity of press briefings at the White House, State Department, and Pentagon in that administration.

Putting politics aside, the 13 individuals make a sound case to hold press briefings on a regular basis. "In any great democracy," they write, "an informed public strengthens the nation. The public has a right to know what its government is doing, and the government has a duty to explain what it is doing."[6]

Further, they state, "The presidents we served believed a better-informed public would be more supportive of the president's policy and political objectives. And a well-informed citizenry would be better equipped to understand the difficult choices and decisions presidents [and other government officials] must make, especially in times of crisis and challenge. Bringing the American people in on the process, early and often, makes for better democracy."[7]

The former spokespersons also argued that in times of military conflict and international crisis, press briefings take on even more importance. Americans want to know the latest developments and seek the truth. One drawback to social media is that it can cause wild rumors to fly. Our adversaries can also manipulate disinformation to their advantage.

Another point they argue is that regular briefings force a certain discipline on government decision making. Knowing there are

briefings scheduled is a powerful incentive for administration officials to complete a policy process on time. Put another way, no president or cabinet secretary wants their spokespersons to say, day after
day, "We haven't quite figured that one out yet." In essence, it keeps
government accountable to those it serves.[8]

The Takeaway

Sometimes just issuing a policy announcement that affects an entire organization is not enough. Whether it is a government agency
with urgent news or a publicly traded company with news about one
of its products, leadership has to stand behind an announcement and
explain it. All organizations—government, corporate, or nonprofit—
have shareholders or stakeholders that have a right to know what is
happening.

Putting a face to the message is sometimes critical. It says the organization is not trying to hide something. Moreover, when there is a
problem—as there was with the Navy and the rash of accidents—having
a leader step up to the microphone conveys, "We are going to fix this."

Notes

1. Hurst and Healy, "Navy Planes Bomb Desert Campground"; and Healy and
Zamichow, "Navy Suspends Operations to Review Safety."
2. Battleship Iowa Museum (website), "Learn the History."
3. Tyler, "Life on Carrier Shows Danger."
4. Author's recollection of events.
5. 13 Former White House Press Secretaries, Foreign Service, and Military Officials,
"Why America Needs to Hear from Its Government."
6. 13 Former White House Press Secretaries.
7. 13 Former White House Press Secretaries.
8. 13 Former White House Press Secretaries.

Chapter 3

The Tailhook Scandal

The Navy's #MeToo Movement in 1991 . . .
And How Leadership Failed Miserably

There are four war-fighting communities in the Navy—surface warfare, submarine warfare, special warfare, and aviation. The surface warfare community is known as the ship drivers, the men and women who man and command the Navy's surface ships—cruisers, destroyers, littoral combatants, and support ships. Surface warfare officers work hard to obtain the qualifications that enable them to stand watch as the officers of the deck—the officers who are the eyes and ears of a ship's captain, and serve as the direct representative when the captain is not on the bridge. Proficiency in navigation, rules of the nautical road, tactical warfare, and shipboard engineering must all be successfully demonstrated to become a qualified surface warfare officer. In the Navy, surface warfare officers are looked upon as "steady as she goes" officers—not glitzy or slick—just solid naval officers.

The submarine community is looked upon as being a bit more cerebral. The men and women who are part of this community serve on nuclear-powered submarines—the "silent service." Becoming a nuclear-trained officer or enlisted submarine sailor is exceptionally demanding. Those who want to become a part of it go through at least two years of schooling and training. Navy nuclear power school is especially demanding. Upon graduation, officers almost become a nuclear engineer. Accordingly, those officers and sailors who are a part of the submarine community are highly respected. What adds to that respect is that many of the Navy's submarines hold 24 nuclear-tipped intercontinental ballistic missiles that are part of our nation's strategic triad.

The special warfare community is more commonly referred to and known as the Navy sea-air-land (SEAL) teams—highly trained war fighters who can operate secretively from the sea, air, or land. All the military services have unique warfare communities; however, the Navy's is the most recognized. Like their counterparts in the other services, SEALs play a prominent role in executing our military strategy in its current geopolitical environment. The nature of warfare has changed, and the unique warfare communities have adapted to each new challenge.

Navy SEALs are highly trained, and their training is tortuous because it has to be. In addition to being physically tough, Navy SEALs are mentally resilient. The conditions they have to operate in are always demanding, and they are often forced to make split-second decisions. The portrayal of Navy SEALs in movies and television shows as being "on the tip of the spear war fighters" is generally accurate. Navy SEALs are part of an elite organization, and the camaraderie found in that community is incredibly strong.

Then there are the naval aviators. There is a range of them, primarily based on the type of aircraft and platforms they fly. The most well-known are the aviators that fly from the decks of the Navy's aircraft carriers and land with the use of a tailhook. At one time, aircraft, such as the F-14, F-4, A-4, A-7, A-6, EA-6B, and the antisubmarine hunter S-3 all flew from the decks of our nation's aircraft carriers. However, today such aircraft are primarily F/A-18 Hornets, new F-35 Lightning IIs, and E-2 Hawkeye early warning planes, in addition to a small number of carrier onboard delivery aircraft that deliver mail, parts, and people to and from the ships. Other naval aviators fly shore-based, fixed-wing aircraft, such as the P-8 antisubmarine warfare plane, while others fly helicopters.

It is the carrier-based aviators that get the notoriety, with their images enhanced from movies like *Top Gun*. That movie introduced audiences to the dangers Navy pilots face—especially when taking off from or landing on aircraft carriers. On a beautiful day at sea, with zero sea state and clear blue skies, getting shot from a catapult and going from zero to 165 miles per hour in two seconds can be a great experience—compared by many to being like an "E-ticket ride" at Disneyland.[1] After completing a mission, pilots return to the ship, coming in at a speed of 150 miles per hour and come to a stop two seconds after catching one of the wires with the tailhook. The skills and training to land a 50,000-ton aircraft on a carrier are not for the faint of heart.

However, not all missions from aircraft carriers occur on days with beautiful, sun-filled blue skies. Many occur at night when the weather is terrible, the seas are mean, the skies are black, and the flight deck is pitching violently. Landing a 50,000-ton aircraft is quite a bit more challenging in those conditions than doing so in ones more favorable. It takes nerves of steel, skill, and countless hours of training and practice.

These skills separate carrier-trained aviators from aviators in the other services. As some say, "there are aviators, and then there are naval aviators."

For whatever reason, carrier-based aviators—the tailhookers—have had more of a propensity to blow off steam or to relax from the demands of their job by enjoying a good party. And a good party, of course, means partaking in alcohol.

Unquestionably, being a tailhook aviator is a unique achievement, and they are clearly in a league of their own. To recognize that fact, active duty naval aviators formed the Tailhook Association in 1956. It eventually grew to become "a private organization composed of active duty, reserve, and retired Navy and Marine Corps aviators, defense contractors, and others."[2] According to Part 1 of the DOD report, *Tailhook 91*:

> The annual Tailhook Symposium began as a reunion of naval aviators in Tijuana, Mexico, in 1956. It was moved to San Diego in 1958 and then to Las Vegas, Nevada, in 1963 where it was expanded to include a number of professional development activities, such as the Flag Panel at which junior officers are given an opportunity to have a candid exchange of questions and answers with flag officers. Official Navy support for the Tailhook Association, especially for the annual convention, also grew. The majority of the planning for the convention's official functions was generally conducted by the office of the Assistant Chief of Naval Operations (Air Warfare). In addition, the Navy provided free office space for the Tailhook Association at Naval Air Station, Miramar, California, and used the Navy's extensive fleet of passenger aircraft to transport attendees to Las Vegas. In 1974, Senator William Proxmire presented his "Golden Fleece Award" to the Navy for using its aircraft to transport attendees to the Tailhook convention in Las Vegas. In 1991, the Navy used some 27 C-9 flights to transport approximately 1,600 people to the convention.
>
> It was also well known throughout the naval aviation community that the annual Tailhook convention was the scene of much drinking, general rowdiness, and wild parties. The 1985 convention caused Vice Admiral Edward H. Martin, then Deputy Chief of Naval Operations (Air Warfare), to write to the Commander, Naval Air Force, Pacific Fleet, asking that he alert his subordinates to a number of concerns.[3]

From 1983 to 1986, I was assigned as the PA officer on the staff of the Naval Air Force, US Pacific Fleet. I was a lieutenant commander, and my boss was Vice Adm Crawford A. "Pete" Easterling. He was a great boss and leader. I learned many lifelong lessons in leadership from him that have remained with me to this day. Easterling—a "tailhooker" himself—was a no-nonsense officer who did not suffer fools and certainly did not tolerate behavior that did not reflect well on the Navy. He never attended a Tailhook convention.

After the 1984 Tailhook convention in Las Vegas, Easterling received a document from the president of the Tailhook Association at the time, then Navy Capt Jack Snyder. Snyder, in his active duty job, was the commanding officer of the Navy Fighter Weapons School—commonly referred to as TOPGUN. In his memo, Snyder documented the behavior he witnessed at the convention. In a word, it was alarmingly inappropriate and indeed not behavior befitting that of US Navy officers. Essentially, Snyder said the behavior at Tailhook must be corrected and could not continue. Easterling immediately forwarded Snyder's concerns, along with his own, to the Pentagon and the head of naval aviation, Vice Adm Ed Martin.

Easterling retired in 1985 and was replaced by then Rear Adm James Service, another carrier-based aviator. Service, just as Easterling had done, sent a similar memo to Martin after the 1985 Tailhook convention. It, too, was an out-of-control event with alarming behavior conducted by naval officers. Like Easterling, Service was most concerned about the potential damage the event could do to the Navy's reputation. It was another warning that something had to be done to fix this "accident waiting to happen."

Martin recast the Service and Easterling memos into one of his own—back to Service—asking him to alert his subordinates to several concerns. The memo read:

> The general decorum and conduct last year [1985] was far less than that expected of mature naval officers. Certain observers even described some of the activity in the hotel halls and suites as grossly appalling, "a rambunctious drunken melee." There was virtually no responsibility displayed by anyone in an attempt to restrain those who were getting out of hand. Heavy drinking and other excesses were not only condoned; they were encouraged by some organizations [Navy aviation squadrons]. We can ill afford this type of behavior and indeed must not tolerate it. The Navy, not the individual, his organization, or the Tailhook Association, is charged with the events and certainly will be cast in disreputable light. Let's get the word out that each individual will be held accountable for his or her actions and also is responsible to exercise common sense and leadership to ensure that his squadron mates and associates conduct themselves with norms expected of naval officers. We will not condone institutionalized indiscretions.[4]

Even a member of the Tailhook Association Board of Directors documented his observations of the 1985 convention in a memo to fellow board members. His memo included these observations:

I viewed with disdain the conduct or better put the misconduct of several officers and a lack of command attention which resulted in damage and imprudent action. . . . The encouragement of drinking contests, the concept of having to drink 15 drinks to win a headband and other related activities produced walking zombies that were viewed by the general public and detracted from the Association/USN [US Navy] integrity. . . . Dancing girls performing lurid sexual acts on naval aviators in public would make prime conversation for the media.[5]

In September 1985, the Tailhook Association Board of Directors had a special meeting to address the behavior contained in that memo. The board member who authored the memo even proposed solutions to excessive drinking and lewd behavior. One solution discussed was the elimination of squadron suites where so much of the inappropriate and lewd behavior occurred. Ironically, the officer who wrote the memo even warned that negative media attention was a distinct possibility.[6] He saw the potential for a possible "train wreck." However, at the next board meeting in October 1985, all the solutions discussed at the September meeting were rejected.[7]

As clear as the warning signs were for leadership to take action and do something to correct the direction of the annual gathering, those signs were ignored. After the initiation and exchange of memos in 1984 and 1985, leadership in the Navy's aviation community had an opportunity to make changes and ensure appropriate behavior and decorum were observed. Unfortunately, they did not pursue this opportunity.

In 1991, events at the convention imploded, causing a massive embarrassment to the Navy and its long and storied history. It was not the proudest time to be wearing a Navy uniform. What happened reflected on everyone who wore the uniform—male or female and at all ranks. It was estimated that attendance at Tailhook '91 was about 5,000. However, only about 2,000 were officially registered. The difference in the numbers stems from the fact that a large portion of military and civilian attendees came for the parties—26 in total—that were being "hosted" in suites on the third floor of the Las Vegas Hilton.[8]

One of the most egregious activities concerned participation in the "gauntlet"—a formation of men who lined the corridor adjacent to the suites at the hotel. According to numerous witness statements, "The gauntlet involved uninvited, assaultive behavior against unsuspecting women entering the third-floor hallway."[9] When Lt Paula Coughlin, a female Navy lieutenant and helicopter pilot—who also happened to be an aide to Rear Adm Jack Snyder—reported that she was assaulted during the gauntlet to Snyder and others in her chain of command, a criminal investigation was initiated.[10] As this story unfolded in the media, other details about what happened at Tailhook 1991 began to emerge. This included not only allegations of sexual assault but also property damage totaling an estimated $23,000.[11]

One has to question the commitment leadership had to solve the problems that were occurring at Tailhook. As documented, there was explicit acknowledgment six or seven years before Tailhook '91 that inappropriate behavior was part of any Tailhook convention. In August 1991, the then president of the Tailhook Association sent a letter to each squadron representative that had booked a suite for the upcoming convention. The letter acknowledged past behavior problems, and the language of the letter also alluded to behavioral issues that were presumed to occur in 1991. A portion of the letter reads, "As last year, you will only be charged for damage inside your suite. The Association will pay for common area damage. In order to keep damage charges to a minimum inside your suite, please make sure you check-in with someone from the Association."[12]

The letter continued, "In the past, we have had a problem with late-night 'gang mentality.' If you see this type of behavior going on, please make an effort to curtail it either by saying something, calling security, or contacting someone from the Association."[13]

The phrase "make an effort to curtail it" does not suggest leadership was taking any decisive steps to address the situation.[14] That type of half-hearted guidance from a Navy captain to junior officers or other attendees appears to encourage bad or even criminal behavior.

The letter continued with, "Remember when bringing in your suite supplies do so with discretion. We are not allowed to bring certain articles into the Hilton. Please cover your supplies by putting them in parachute bags or boxes. DO NOT BORROW LAUNDRY BASKETS FROM THE HILTON. THEIR SENSE OF HUMOR DOES NOT GO THAT FAR!!!"[15] That guidance is further reinforcement and condoning of unsavory and illegal behavior.

After Lieutenant Coughlin's allegations of assault made their way up the chain of command, other media reports about what had happened at Tailhook '91 soon began to emerge, and the Navy launched its first investigation into the convention. This report concluded that the incident was mainly the fault of some junior officers who had behaved poorly.

The Assistant Secretary of the Navy for Manpower and Reserve Affairs, Barbara Pope, refused to accept the results of this investigation. Influencing her decision not to accept the report stemmed, in part, from the head of the Naval Investigative Service (NIS), Rear Adm Duval Williams, who said in Pope's presence that he believed that "a lot of female Navy pilots are go-go dancers, topless dancers or hookers."[16]

When Williams issued his final report, finding that none of the senior Navy officials bore responsibility for what occurred in Las Vegas, Pope went to Secretary of the Navy Larry Garrett and told him that she would resign if the Navy did not "do another report and look at what we needed to do about accountability and responsibility and the larger issues at hand."[17] Pope correctly saw that the Navy's report was inadequate. Accordingly, Garrett agreed with Pope, and a further investigation was conducted, this one directed by the DOD and headed by Derek J. Vander Schaaf, the Inspector General (IG) of the DOD. Embarrassingly, the investigation was taken out of the Navy's hands.

Vander Schaaf's report was released in September 1992. In his opening remarks, Vander Schaaf states:

> Misconduct at the 1991 Tailhook Symposium was more widespread than previously reported by the Navy. We identified 90 victims of indecent assault. In addition, we documented a significant number of incidents of indecent exposure, and other types of sexual misconduct, as well as other improprieties by Navy and Marine Corps officers. We established that more than 50 officers made false statements to us during the investigation.[18]

Vander Schaaf concluded that there were violations of law and regulation, and there was not any accountability for the leadership failures that occurred at Tailhook. In his view, "The deficiencies in the investigation were the result of an attempt to limit the exposure of the Navy and senior Navy officials to criticism regarding Tailhook 91."[19]

The release of the report led to the resignations of Rear Adm John E. Gordon, Judge Advocate General of the Navy, and Rear Admiral Williams.[20] *Frontline* reported, "Ultimately, the careers of fourteen admirals and almost 300 naval aviators were scuttled or damaged by Tailhook. For example, Secretary of the Navy H. Lawrence Garrett III and CNO Adm Frank Kelso were both at Tailhook '91. Consequently, Garrett resigned, and Kelso retired early two years after the convention."[21] Vice Adm Richard Dunleavy, the Deputy CNO for Air Warfare, was demoted to the rank of two-star admiral (from a three-star admiral) and retired because of the scandal.[22]

Vander Schaaf's two-volume report is graphic—including words of caution to readers because of the language and photos in the report.

In the foreword, he states, "It is important to understand that the events at Tailhook 91 did not occur in a historical vacuum. Similar behavior had occurred at previous conventions. The emerging pattern of some of the activities, such as the gauntlet, began to assume the aura of 'tradition.' There is some evidence to suggest that Tailhook 91 was 'tame' in comparison to earlier conventions."[23]

Nevertheless, the critical point is that the behavior that occurred at Tailhook should have never happened. Leadership should have stepped in years before and said: "**STOP. This type of behavior will not be tolerated. If you behave this way and participate in such behavior, you will be severely punished and separated from the Navy.**"

The Vander Schaaf report documented numerous failures on the part of the Navy and its leadership. In addition to documenting specific instances of assault and criminal behavior, some of the other glaring observations included:

- In the Navy's initial investigation, the Navy's IG did not interview senior officials who were at Tailhook '91. These officers should have been interviewed to determine criminal activity or misconduct or to assign responsibility for any misconduct there.[24]

- The Navy IG felt that if he did interview senior officials who were at Tailhook '91, it would be perceived as a witch-hunt.[25]

- In the Navy IG report, a common thread running through an overwhelming majority of interviews was, "What's the big deal?"[26]

- The commander of the then NIS, Rear Adm Williams, was reluctant to interview one particular admiral on the existence of the gauntlet. He declined because he felt it was outside the scope of his organization. NIS is now referred to as the Naval Criminal Investigative Service (NCIS) and is the primary law enforcement arm of both the Navy and Marine Corps. Its primary purpose is to investigate criminal activity—just as it does in the television show that carries its name.

- The NIS commander stated his feelings about NIS's role in the investigation by saying NIS did not have "a fart's chance in a whirlwind" of solving it.[27]

- The NIS Regional Director for the National Capital Region stated to Vander Schaaf's investigators that "he was under constant pressure from NIS headquarters, specifically the director of NIS, to close the investigation."[28]

- NIS, in the course of its role in the investigation, did not afford the Navy IG's team access to complete information.[29] How could that possibly happen? How could these two organizations not work together? Possibly because of internal bickering resulting from an inspection of NIS by the Navy IG in August 1991—a situation that should have been easily solved by good leadership.

- The Navy Judge Advocate General did not play a role in ensuring the Navy investigations were adequate in addressing all relevant issues, including accountability of misconduct.[30]

As a result of these failures and others, the Navy's leadership failed all who ever wore the Navy uniform. The effect on morale ran deep—not just in the naval aviation community but in every other part of the Navy as well. Headlines stemming from the Navy's inadequate investigation and Vander Schaaf's in-depth report continued for over two years and were amplified by the Navy's inability to police itself. The term *Tailhook* is still associated with instances of sexual assault. However, despite the negative publicity and morale problems that Tailhook caused, some argue that the Navy and the entire military—in a sordid way—may have benefited from it.

Robert L. Beck, a retired Navy captain and naval aviator, was an attendee at Tailhook '91. In 2016, Beck published *Inside the Tailhook Scandal: A Naval Aviator's Story*.[31] In that same year, he also wrote a newspaper column in which he argues that since Tailhook '91, "There have been monumental cultural and institutional changes in naval aviation, the Navy, and the Armed Forces . . . Tailhook played a major role in changing the Pentagon's Combat Exclusion Policy. In 1993, women could serve in almost any aviation capacity. Also, new legislation allowed women to serve on combat ships."[32] Beck concluded:

In [the] ensuing years, women continued to break new ground in the military. Their performance in Operations Iraqi and Enduring Freedom, following the 9/11 attacks, was a critical factor in the Pentagon decision to lift restrictions on some 14,000 positions—although women were still excluded from 20 percent of all military positions.

In 2013, Secretary of Defense Leon Panetta removed the ban on women in combat. The final restrictions were lifted by Secretary of Defense Ash [Ashton] Carter, who announced that all combat positions would be open to women beginning in 2016, and . . . [in March 2016] approved final plans by all the armed services to open up all positions.[33]

Also, female applicants to the US Naval Academy increased, and the mandatory sensitivity training that resulted from Tailhook is a model that other organizations have used as a baseline.

However, the fact remains that even though there were 90 victims of sexual assault at Tailhook '91, authorities did not initiate any court-martials. Yes, scores of careers were ruined or ended prematurely, but Tailhook—over many years—represented a total failure of leadership. Long before Tailhook '91, prudent officers stayed away from the convention because they knew what was going to happen there.

After Tailhook '91, some naval aviation officers even designed a flight suit patch that said: "TAILHOOK 91—I didn't do it! Nobody Saw Me Do It—You Can't Prove a Thing! I WASN'T THERE."[34] Some would argue that the patch was designed and worn by those who did not attend Tailhook. Conversely, others would argue it was designed by aviators that *were* there but who denied participating in or seeing any poor behavior.

Vander Schaaf's report documents a few officers reporting the existence of two groups that were described as an allegiance among officers. The rules for the group were based around the fact that "a junior officer will not 'give up' another junior officer just because he had done 'something stupid.'"[35] Regardless of these facts, some claimed Tailhook '91 was a total success. This is evidenced in a letter from the Tailhook Association president in October 1991: "Without a doubt, this was the biggest and most successful Tailhook we have ever had. We said it would be the 'Mother of all Hooks' and it was. . . . Additionally, all of our naval aviation leaders and main industry leaders had nothing but praise for the event."[36] Then in his third paragraph, he documented the damage that occurred in some of the suites, as well as the existence of the gauntlet tradition.[37]

Nonetheless, regardless of what Navy leadership knew about what happened at Tailhook conventions—criminal behavior in the form of sexual assault, debauchery, failed leadership, and overall inappropriate behavior—Tailhook conventions were supported as a legitimate professional development seminar. The bottom-line lesson, both for communicators and organizational leaders, is to have the courage to do the right thing when a problem happens—step in, raise your hand, and say this is going to hurt the organization and say **"STOP!"**

During my career, I commonly did a "sniff test" with many issues—if it does not look right or "smell right," it most likely will not pass muster with the media, Congress, your employees, your shareholders, or other stakeholders. Not passing your personal sniff test is often an indication that whatever program, effort, or initiative you or your organization may be considering is not a good idea. Being able to have that "gut" instinct is an attribute all excellent communicators and leaders must learn to develop.

When a communicator must speak on someone else's behalf and has knowledge that the individual mentioned tolerates less than admirable or criminal behavior, the job becomes much more difficult. The worst thing a communicator can do is lie. A communicator is only as good as the information provided by leadership. Moreover, if your leadership hides behind the truth or fails to act appropriately, it is a recipe for disaster.

Fortunately, in the case of Tailhook conventions, there were people in the Navy who knew the "ground truth" and what was happening. They dared to come forward and disclose to the media what had happened at Tailhook '91. The *San Diego Union* was the leader in covering the convention. Reporter Gregory Vistica did an incredible job of reporting the events that took place that year in Las Vegas. He was nominated for a Pulitzer Prize and was awarded the George Polk Award for exposing the unacceptable and criminal behavior displayed by naval officers at Tailhook '91, and the Navy's failure to investigate itself.[38] As a result of his reporting, Vistica quickly earned a reputation—at least in the eyes of some Navy leaders—as someone who wanted to take the Navy down and do it harm. This reaction to the media is certainly not unique and is often the response of the leadership of any organization that comes under fire by the media.

Although Vistica's work helped lead to massive changes in the Navy and its acceptance of women, those changes should not have evolved in the way they did. Tailhook '91 greatly tarnished the image of the Navy by failed leadership—leadership that knew right from wrong but chose to turn a blind eye to reality.

As Vander Schaaf so well states, "The 'Tailhook 'traditions' (the gauntlet, ballwalking, leg shaving, mooning, streaking, and lewd sexual conduct) so deviated from the standards of behavior the nation expects of its military officers that the repetition of this behavior year after year raises serious questions about the senior leadership of the Navy."[39] Although organizers of Tailhook '91 encouraged "duty officers" to oversee activity in the Hilton suites, the presence of sober officers should not have been necessary to warn of possible poor behavior.

Leaders tolerated the culture of Tailhook Association participants—from aviation squadron commanders to flag officers (admirals). The blame should be shared with them. The damage suffered to the Navy's image as a result of years of inappropriate Tailhook behavior has taken many years to repair. Additionally, it has caused further damage, to both future naval aviators and those women attempting to break into the ranks of those who furthered the "Tailhook culture."[40]

The Takeaway

The key to any crisis is how an organization handles or deals with the situation, and it is clear the Navy did not handle the Tailhook crisis very well. It handled it abysmally. The fact that the DOD had to step in do a separate investigation of the 1991 Tailhook convention—in essence, dismissing the Navy's efforts—was shameful.

An essential element of good leadership is integrity, and the Navy did not react with integrity before, during or after Tailhook '91. Good leaders see problems before they become crises and have the courage to do something about such issues. In today's parlance, "If you see something, do something."

And leaders see problems by being engaged. Failure to be engaged—to "hear no evil or speak no evil,'" to think about the "good ol' days," to hope those "good ol' days" will return by "circling the wagons," and to go into denial—is cause for concern. Tailhook '91 damaged personal lives and ruined careers of many outstanding individuals, not to mention the damage to the Navy's reputation. Tailhook and its innuendo are still referred to today in articles, books, and seminars about sexual harassment.

Tailhook '91 and previous Tailhook conferences were a crisis the Navy allowed to happen because leadership did not have courage, was not engaged, and chose to "circle the wagons."

I find a similar comparison to Tailhook behavior with the controversies that have surrounded the Catholic Church with its priests engaging in sexual abuse and predatory behavior. Leadership in the Catholic Church—very similar to leadership in the Navy—has turned a blind eye to what they have known for decades. They choose instead to cover up what they know is criminal behavior and have not had courage to end it.

Communications professional Andrea Obston contends there are two types of crises: (1) emergencies that are often not the fault of anyone and (2) chronic problems that lead to a crisis. Tailhook was clearly in the second category. As Obston argues, chronic-type problems are worse because they can erupt if unattended. They are made worse by the fact that an organization should have known what was going to happen and should have done something about it.[41] For Tailhook '91, the "writing was on the wall."

Navy leaders that allowed such unseemly and dangerous behavior to continue at annual Tailhook conventions reflected arrogance, and arrogance does not have a place in any leadership position. Crisis communications expert Jim Lukaszewski argues that arrogant leaders go into denial and encourage subordinates not to overreact. Instead, they begin the search for other "guilty" parties. For example, the media or disgruntled organization insiders chose to blow the whistle on things they perceived to be problems.[42] Lukaszewski captures the concepts of arrogance, denial, and shifting blame as having a case of Testosterosis—and the naval aviation community had enough testosterone to go around.[43] Many individuals caught the illness of Tailhook.

Tailhook was a costly lesson for the Navy. Other organizations should take heed and learn from it.

Notes

1. An E ticket (officially an E coupon) was a type of admission ticket used at the Disneyland and Magic Kingdom theme parks before 1982, where it admitted the bearer to the newest, most advanced, or popular rides and attractions. See Wikipedia, "E Ticket."

2. Department of Defense (DOD), *Tailhook 91*, Part 1, 1.

3. DOD, *Tailhook 91*, Part 1, 2. "The term [Flag officer] as used in this report applies to Navy admirals and Marine Corps general officers."

4. DOD, *Tailhook 91*, Part 1, 2.

5. DOD, *Tailhook 91*, Part 1, 3.

6. DOD, *Tailhook 91*, Part 2, V-2.

7. DOD, *Tailhook 91*, Part 2, V-3.

8. DOD, *Tailhook 91*, Part 1, 3–4.

9. DOD, *Tailhook 91*, Part 2, VI-1.

10. DOD, *Tailhook 91*, Part 1, 4. Of note, the now Rear Adm Jack Snyder was the same Jack Snyder who, as a captain and commanding officer of TOPGUN and for-

mer president of the Tailhook Association, wrote the memo in 1984 warning of the poor behavior he observed at Tailhook that year.

11. DOD, *Tailhook 91,* Part 1, 5.
12. DOD, *Tailhook 91,* Part 1, Enclosure 2.
13. DOD, Encl. 2.
14. DOD, Encl. 2.
15. DOD, Encl. 2.
16. DOD, Encl. 15.
17. McMichael, *Mother of All Hooks,* 273.
18. DOD, cover memo.
19. DOD, *Tailhook 91,* Part 2, cover memo.
20. Healy, "Pentagon Blasts Tailhook Probe."
21. "Tailhook '91," PBS *Frontline.*
22. Lewis, "Tailhook Affair Brings Censure of 3 Admirals."
23. DOD, *Tailhook 91,* Part 2, i.
24. DOD, *Tailhook 91,* Part 1, 8.
25. DOD, 8.
26. DOD, 10.
27. DOD, 18.
28. DOD, 18.
29. DOD, 18.
30. DOD, 19.
31. Beck, *Inside the Tailhook Scandal.*
32. Beck, "How Navy Has Changed Since Tailhook."
33. Beck, "Tailhook Started Huge Changes."
34. Vistica, *Fall from Glory,* 362.
35. DOD, *Tailhook 91,* Part 2, IV-2.
36. DOD, *Tailhook 91,* Part 1, Enclosure 3.
37. DOD, *Tailhook 91,* Part 1, Enclosure 3.
38. Vistica, *Fall from Glory.*
39. DOD, *Tailhook 91,* Part 2, X-5.
40. Spears, *Call Sign Revlon.*
41. Obston, "Crisis Public Relations Basic Training."
42. Lukaszewski, "Strengthening Corporate Trust," 11–12.
43. Lukaszewski, 12.

Chapter 4

Examples of How Not to Conduct Business with the Media

The Voice Mail Guidance

After 31 pressure-packed years in the Navy and eight-plus at Lockheed Martin corporate headquarters in Bethesda, Maryland, it was time for a change of pace—especially after spending several months out of the workplace supporting my wife as she dealt with a serious medical issue. However, after the medical issue was resolved and life returned to normal, I saw a position advertised for the Chief of Corporate Communications at the US Mint headquarters in Washington, DC, and I became rather enthusiastic. This sounded like a fun job, and when I met the Director of the Mint, Edmund Moy, as part of the interview process, I knew it would be a good fit. I joined the Mint in 2009.

Moy and I hit it off quickly, and it did turn out to be a fun and interesting job. Moy was a political appointee and was named the director of the Mint by Pres. George W. Bush. Moy had served in the White House with President Bush and came to the Mint afterwards. However, when the Obama administration took office, anyone with an "R" (Republican) after his or her name was not well accepted as a member of the new administration's team. Those who had a "D" (Democrat) fared much better. Nevertheless, the Director of the Mint is a five-year appointed position, and Moy wanted to serve a full term. He departed in 2011 after standing up well to the Obama-infused Treasury Department leadership (the US Mint is part of the Treasury Department).

The leadership team at Treasury—at least those who made up the PA staff—was quite young and inexperienced. They were perhaps very "book smart," but they did not have the hands-on work and life experience to go along with their "smarts." Most were political appointees, by the way.

After Moy left, the Mint was led by Richard Peterson, a career public servant. Peterson was given the job in an acting capacity, pending the appointment of a White House nominee. Peterson served in that position for about four years—an unprecedented amount of time to serve in a government position in an acting capacity. When the White House finally named an appointee in 2015, the public announcement was handled in an awkward and unprofessional way.

There was clearly a difference in opinion at the Treasury Department and the White House over who that nominee should be. Mr. Rhett Jeppson, already a political appointee at the Small Business Administration, was the choice of some individuals at Treasury and ultimately the White House nominee.

At the Mint we were given an announcement that we could use in communicating with our employees about the newly nominated director. Those at Treasury who were not supportive of the Jeppson selection were told they could not make edits to the announcement. I was personally told not to confirm Jeppson's name if it were to leak ahead of the announcement. I was also told to inform Treasury PA if I received any media calls before the announcement.

When the US Mint released the internal email and it was sent to the 1,800 US Mint employees, I quickly received a phone call from one of the trade publication reporters who covered the Mint. He happened to be at a trade show in Florida, and several Mint employees were also there representing our bureau. When the employees saw the announcement on their computers and hand-held devices, they mentioned the news to the reporter. The reporter immediately called me for confirmation—which I provided to him.

I then proceeded to call Treasury PA to inform the office that at least one member of the trade media was aware of the new director's being named.

To my surprise—and shock actually—the individual whom I informed went ballistic. When I told the individual (a political appointee) what had transpired and that I had confirmed what was in the email, the individual shouted: "Why did you do that? I told you I wanted you to call me if you received any media queries."

I actually had the individual on speakerphone with two members of my staff present with me because I had grown to distrust this staff member's guidance, and I simply did not like the all too frequent surly, arrogant attitude.

I told the staff member there was nothing classified in the announcement and that it had been sent to all 1,800 Mint employees. The staffer then said something that shocked me and the two staff members: "If you receive any more media calls on this issue, **send them to voice mail**."

I told the staffer that if I did what she was suggesting—to send reporters to voice mail—the many mentors I have had over the years would roll over in their graves.

My staff members—my deputy and my special assistant who were both seasoned communicators with decades of experience in media relations—were aghast. To send media calls to voice mail over such a simple issue was beyond belief. Guidance such as this violates every rule in the book about how to deal with the media. My two colleagues had a good laugh after I hung up the phone. We also shook our heads together in disbelief and wondered how the Treasury Department was handling other far more complicated and sensitive issues.

I then proceeded to call the other trade publications that covered us to let them know of the announcement about a new director being nominated. Since I had already confirmed this to one news outlet, it was only proper to quickly do the same with the other trade reporters that covered the US Mint.

The Penny and CBS's *Sunday Morning*

One of the issues that continued to come up at the Mint was the penny. A constant question from both the media and the public was why we continued to produce a penny that cost almost twice as much to manufacture than it was worth? Many countries had done away with their version of the penny, with Canada being one of them. When the Canadians eliminated its penny from production, its government did a great job of explaining to the Canadian citizenry how they were going to implement the elimination. I had numerous conversations with my Canadian counterpart, and I felt prepared to copycat the Canadian plan if the decision to eliminate the penny in the United States was ever made. In simple terms, what the Canadian plan called for was rounding off purchases to the nearest five or zero digits. In other words, if an item were to cost $1.02, the merchant would charge the customer $1.00. If the item were to cost $1.03, the merchant would round it up to $1.05.

My Canadian counterpart provided me their communications plan and all the materials they used to explain why and how they were undertaking the effort. The Canadians executed the plan seamlessly and there were not any repercussions for the government.

That was good for our northern neighbors. However, the bottom line in the United States was that our political leadership in the US did not dare to pull the trigger and do away with the penny coin. Those of us at the Mint would often say to ourselves during internal discussions that if we were a private company and we were making a product that cost almost twice to make as we sold it for (the US Mint sells all its coins to the Federal Reserve at face value), our president and chief executive officer (CEO) would be fired.

However, "Washington remains Washington," and this means bureaucracy, politics, and political influence. The maker of the penny blanks, for example, was a company called Jarden Zinc Products based in Greeneville, Tennessee. Whenever the talk of eliminating the penny came up, the company mobilized its political base and its lobbyists.

In 2014, a producer from the CBS-TV magazine called CBS's *Sunday Morning* called and requested a visit to the Philadelphia Mint. Philadelphia and Denver are the two facilities that produce the nation's circulating coins. The producer indicated they were interested in doing a piece on the penny and why it cost almost twice as much to produce as it was worth. In fact, at the time, it cost more than twice as much: 2.4 cents.

Because the call was from a national media organization, we called Treasury PA and informed them of the request. We were prepared to accommodate the request, and we wanted to inform the Treasury. The response from my counterpart there was a curt and straightforward "No. We really don't want them doing this story. The time is not right."

My staff and I were somewhat miffed, but we came up with an excuse every time the producer would call back to check on his request: "Philadelphia is undergoing an audit"; "We're preparing our annual report to Congress and can't accommodate your request right now;" or "Philadelphia is undergoing some maintenance, and a visit just won't work at this time."

Finally, after several months of stalling and finding every excuse in the book, I jokingly told the acting Director of the Mint—Dick Peterson—that my nose was growing longer every day, and it was about to fall off.

So I asked Peterson if he would bring the CBS request up at his next meeting with the Treasurer of the United States, Rosie Rios. My Treasury counterpart had convinced Rios that accommodating the request was not a good idea, but when Peterson came back from his meeting, he informed me that we had a green light. I was delighted to call the producer and inform him of the news. We set a date and time for the Philadelphia visit, and all was finally on track. There was not a reason for blocking *CBS Sunday Morning* from doing its story. The TV story was slated to be presented by Mo Rocca, an excellent reporter who always seemed to lighten things up with his upbeat demeanor.

I prepared a set of talking points that I was going to use in discussing the penny's continued production and use with Rocca. My last point was that the US Mint made the one-cent coin because our customer, the Federal Reserve, kept asking for it. Moreover, it was our job to meet our customer's demands. I also noted that the Mint did not create policies—we only executed them. In other words, if Treasury, the White House, or even Congress told us to stop making the penny, we would. It was not our decision.

I was actually in my car on my way to Philadelphia to prepare for the visit by CBS. Halfway up the Baltimore-Washington Parkway, Peterson called me. When I saw his number come up on my phone, I suddenly had a bad feeling. I could not have been more instinctive.

"Tom, come on back to the office. Treasury has cold feet, and they're pulling the plug on CBS," Peterson said.

"Dick, the producer, is going to go crazy. I've been stalling this guy for months. They've made all sorts of arrangements with Rocca and their crew," I said. "What do I tell him?"

I pulled over to the side of the road, took a deep breath, and called the producer. I knew what his reaction was going to be, and I held the phone away from my ear as I told him about the most recent decision. He did not disappoint. He was angry—actually livid—and I did not blame him.

After he calmed down somewhat, I asked him if I could go "off the record" and explain the situation. I explained what was happening and why Treasury was reticent about doing the story. It was politics— plain and simple. I told him that if CBS wanted to do the story without us, they certainly could. We could provide them b-roll footage (background video) of the penny being produced as we always had that available for all our various coin denominations. CBS could go to our annual report and see the latest cost figures of all our coin productions, and it indeed could find talking heads (not associated with the government) to argue both sides of the issue.

The whole ordeal was simply a perfect storm of how not to handle a media relations situation—especially as a government entity. The public has a right to know how and why its money is being spent. I consider it a travesty when government employees—be they political appointees or career service—refuse to come clean with those whom they serve. In this case, I consider the Treasury's actions dishonest, unethical, and just plain shameful.

Despite how leadership at the Treasury handled the matter, the show itself was and remains extremely entertaining, very informative, and well-produced. It is undoubtedly not hard-hitting like *60 Minutes* can be.

The Dollar Coin Versus the Dollar Bill

We faced a somewhat similar situation with the dollar bill. Although the US Mint does not produce paper currency (we only produced coins), our sister agency—the Bureau of Engraving and Printing—does. The Mint, however, produced the $1 coin. At the time, we could produce the coin for about 18 cents and sell it to the Federal Reserve at face value—one dollar. This would mean a profit of about 82 cents—money that would be returned to the Treasury and the American taxpayer. The dime and quarter coins were also produced for much less than face value—the dime for about three cents and the quarter for about eight cents.

When those coins are monetized—or sold to the Federal Reserve at their face value—the difference is returned to the Treasury General Fund at the end of the FY. In FY 2017, for example, the Mint returned approximately $422 million to the Treasury. This included profit from circulating coin production and "profit" from sales of numismatic products.[1] The government dislikes the use of the term profit, but there is not another way to succinctly explain why and how that money benefits the taxpayer and how it is transferred from the Mint to the Treasury Department. The term that we officially used to describe the difference between the production cost of a coin and its face value is seigniorage. That is a tough word for the public to get its head around, but profit is a much better way for the layman to understand the concept. At the same time, the cost to produce the penny in FY 2017 was 1.8 cents and the nickel 6.6 cents. That is a loss in "profit" for the Mint and the taxpayer.

So imagine how the US taxpayer would benefit from using a dollar coin instead of a dollar bill. Let us speak very conservatively and say the US Mint produced two billion dollar coins each year and delivered them to the Federal Reserve. (The 2018 plan was for the Bureau of Engraving and Printing to produce 2.2 billion one-dollar notes). The Treasury General Fund, and ultimately the taxpayer, would benefit by approximately $360 million. This would be a very handsome return, even though it costs more than the face value to produce both the penny and the nickel.

The United States is one of the few countries—if not the only country—that still uses the dollar bill. Canada did away with its dollar bill many years ago, as did European countries that use the Euro. Other major countries include Great Britain and Japan. These countries use the much more cost-effective dollar coin equivalent. Due to the presence of an image of a loon on the coin, Canadians call their dollar coin a Loonie and even produce a two-dollar equivalent they call a double Loonie.[2] These countries find it hard to believe that we still produce the dollar bill. It is expensive to produce and does not have a long shelf life. While a dollar bill may last up to four years, a coin can last 35 to 50 years.

However, the same situation in the United States that exists with the penny also exists with the dollar coin. Whenever there is talk about doing away with the dollar bill, our political leadership backs away. Also, a company called Crane Paper Company, headquartered in Massachusetts, puts its congressional delegation, lobbyists, and PR machine into overdrive to thwart the efforts. Crane has been the sole supplier of currency paper to the US Government since engraver Paul Revere began printing money for the colonies.

Once again, all our political leadership has to do is step up to the plate and make a decision that will benefit the taxpayer. Contrary to what some may think, the American public is smart. If you explain to the consumer and taxpayer why you are making a decision—especially a decision that makes sense, saves money, and increases efficiency—the taxpayer will understand.

During my tenure at the Mint, I met with many of my counterparts from other countries, and they all, without exception, said you cannot give people a choice when it comes to the equivalent of the dollar bill or the dollar coin. If you do, they will always resort to the "old way" of doing things. Change (no pun intended) is hard. However, if you have the political courage to do what is right and explain that decision, the public will support you. In addition to doing the right thing, it is also a matter of integrity. When will the US political leadership have the courage to do the right thing? In this case, when will our political leaders make the decision to do away with the dollar bill and use dollar coins instead?

Congress legislates all coins, and the dollar coin is not an exception. The US Mint started producing one in 1979. Derisively referred to as the "Carter quarter" in reference to high inflation that dogged the administration and called the Susan B. Anthony, it was poorly designed in that it too closely resembled the size of a quarter. Many people found it hard to distinguish from the quarter because of this size, along with similar color and reeded (ridged) edges that also appear on the quarter. Production ended in 1999.

The Sacagawea dollar coin was introduced in 2000 with the same result. It too closely resembled the quarter—this time even though it was gold in color, it was still the same size as the quarter.[3] Other Native American and Presidential dollar coins followed with the same basic composition. People found it easier to stay with the dollar bill.

While these coins were being produced—billions of them—we were also producing billions of dollar bills. When given a choice between using a dollar bill or a dollar coin that resembled a quarter, people chose to stay the course and use the dollar bill. You really could not blame the public for making this choice. Consequently, the Federal Reserve banks found themselves with nearly one and a half billion one-dollar coins stacked in their vaults around the country. The Federal Reserve was growing exasperated with having to store them—made even worse because it knew there was never going to be a demand for the coins.

In 2011, the Treasury Department began an effort to eliminate the dollar coin—and perhaps thought to close some Mint facilities around the country. The Mint has facilities in Philadelphia, Denver, West Point, New York, and San Francisco—along with its headquarters in Washington, DC. When the financial crisis hit in 2008, the demand to produce coins diminished markedly. People were not spending money, and people were emptying piggy banks and using their saved coins in everyday transactions. Consequently, those coins were finding their way back into circulation after being used, precluding a need to make new ones.

A good barometer of how well the economy was doing is to look at the amount of circulating coins the Mint was producing. In FY 2009, the Mint produced 5.2 billion coins. This number reflected the recession and was a 45-year low for coin production. As a matter of comparison, the Mint produced more than 12 billion coins in FY 2019, clearly reflecting an improved economy.

As the midterm elections approached in 2012, the Obama administration was looking for ways to showcase some of its accomplishments. Congress passed the Affordable Care Act in 2010, but its major provisions were not going into effect until 2014. With two years under its belt, the administration began to ponder things it could showcase to the taxpayer—efficiencies and actions they had taken as good stewards of the taxpayer. President Obama had signed an Executive Order establishing the Campaign to Cut Government Waste, charging federal agencies to scour their operations from top to bottom for ways to streamline government and cut costs.[4] After two years in office, it was time for the administration to document what it had done.

One thing initially considered by the Treasury Department was closing two Mint facilities—Denver and San Francisco. Acting Mint Director Peterson met with Treasury Department leadership and he asked Treasury leadership if such an action was politically prudent. He asked, "Did they really want to close the San Francisco Mint in Congresswoman Pelosi's district or close the Mint in Denver where half our circulating coins are produced, not to mention Colorado's being a swing state at the time?"

The political appointees at the Treasury Department saw the value in those arguments and chose to go in a different direction. Instead of closing two Mint facilities, they chose a more straightforward route—eliminating the one-dollar coin. Accordingly, the Mint was directed to prepare a memorandum that outlined the impact of such an action. Treasury officials then proceeded to tell the Office of Management and Budget (OMB) that eliminating the dollar coin would not have a financial impact on the US Mint's seigniorage (profit). The Treasury argument was a very shortsighted one. Not producing the coin would preclude the Treasury from building a special warehouse for the 1.5 billion dollar coins that were in the inventory. The cost of the warehouse would be $600,000. Therefore, that would be the savings.

The problem with this commitment by Treasury to OMB was that it was not valid. Not producing the dollar coin *would* have a financial impact on the US Mint—and ultimately, the taxpayer. The Mint's chief financial officer (CFO), David Motl—a career civil servant with unsurpassed integrity—distinctly told the Treasury Department and

OMB that there *would* be financial repercussions. Conservatively speaking, $360 million was being returned to the taxpayer every year the dollar coin was produced and used in place of the dollar bill.

Nevertheless, in December 2011, the Treasury Department made the decision to cease production of the dollar coin that was intended for circulation. At a White House event, Vice Pres. Joe Biden and Neal Wolin, the deputy secretary of the Treasury, announced ceasing the production of the circulating dollar coins. They announced the cease in production at an event tied to results from the Campaign to Cut Government Waste.

The truth of the matter is that it was a poor decision—and one easier to make instead of one that would significantly benefit the taxpayer. The correct decision would have been to eliminate the dollar bill. Again, explaining such a decision to the American citizen would resonate. Saving taxpayers' money always does. However, grandstanding at the White House in a press conference and photo op about cutting government waste appears to make sense to taxpayers when they do not know any better.

In a blog posting by Wolin explaining the decision, he referred to several congressional members who had expressed concerns about a large number of dollar coins stored in Federal Reserve vaults. To me, that translated to pressure on congressional members from lobbyists who had an interest in keeping the dollar bill. Wolin failed to mention the many congressional members from both sides of the aisle that favored eliminating the dollar bill and using the dollar coin. One of the senators who introduced legislation supporting the dollar coin was Senator John McCain.

In 10 separate reports over 24 years, the nonpartisan Government Accountability Office (GAO) recommended switching to the dollar coin. The GAO estimates switching would save the government a minimum of $150 million per year and $4.4 billion over 30 years.[5] Additionally, endorsements for switching to the dollar coin have come from several newspapers and media outlets. These include the *New York Times*, the *Washington Post*, the *Boston Globe, Los Angeles Times, Chicago Tribune, USA Today, and* the *Denver Post*, among others.[6]

Perhaps the taxpayer would have been better served if Wolin had given thought to John Adam's perspective on coinage. In a letter to Thomas Jefferson in 1787, Adams said, "All the perplexities, confusions, and distress in America arise, not from defects in their constitution or confederation, not from want of honor or virtue, so much as from the downright ignorance of the nature of coin, credit, and circulation."[7]

Sometimes making the "easy" decision translates into a decision that lacks integrity. Furthermore, sometimes the story behind the story is more interesting. However, you must have a free and open press to look into issues because what the public sees is not always what they get.

The term "fake news" has received much attention in the media. Fake news is "fabricated information that mimics news media content in form but not in organizational process or intent. Fake news outlets, in turn, lack the news media's editorial norms and processes for ensuring the accuracy and credibility of information. Fake news overlaps with other information disorders, such as misinformation (false or misleading information) and disinformation (false information that is purposely spread to deceive people)."[8] Regardless of its true meaning, "fake news" has now come to mean what politicians and media critics use to describe stories about which they may not agree. Nevertheless, the fact of the matter is that an open and free press is the foundation of democracy. It is a tenet upon which our country was built. The fruits of an open and free press are endless.

Examples include the mistreatment of our wounded servicemen at Walter Reed Medical Center uncovered by the *Washington Post*; the negligent care of our veterans at the Veterans Hospital in Phoenix and other Veterans Administration hospitals; the Tailhook scandal uncovered by the *San Diego Union*; the Watergate scandal relentlessly pursued by the *Washington Post*; the disclosure of child molestation by an assistant football coach at Pennsylvania State University by the *Harrisburg Patriot-News*; the initial disclosure of child sexual abuse by Roman Catholic priests in the Boston area by the *Boston Globe* that led to the award-winning movie *Spotlight*; disclosure of the *Pentagon Papers* by the *New York Times*; and the exoneration of four black men on murder charges (two of whom were awaiting execution) after three journalism students from Northwestern University and *Chicago Lawyer* magazine pursued their cases. The list goes on endlessly.

Do we as communicators and our leaders like every story we see? Of course not. Nevertheless, a free and open press is one of the fruits we enjoy every day. The best thing we can do is to work with the media representatives who cover us. You do not have to make them your best friends; however, it is to our advantage as a spokesman and

organization—and the media's too—to establish good, sound relationships that enhance trust and credibility. Moreover, when bad news
hits your organization, which it inevitably will, you are one step ahead
of the game by at least having media representatives whom you trust
and who trust you.

And the "L" Word . . . the Aftermath of Telling a Lie Has Consequences

As previously mentioned, I was assigned to the staff of the Naval
Air Force, US Pacific Fleet from 1983 to 1986. We were headquartered at the North Island Naval Air Station in Coronado, California,
across the bay from San Diego. I was driving home from work on the
evening of 10 January 1985, when something strange happened. The
city lights went out as a massive power outage hit San Diego County.
I remember listening to radio station KFMB, a top-rated station because of its news, traffic, and weather reports. They were covering the
outage but were unable to say what caused it. The weather had been
excellent, and there were not any reports of traffic accidents that
might have caused the problem. I was as perplexed as everyone.

Later that evening, I started to receive phone calls from the San
Diego media, asking if the Navy had been conducting any exercises
where it might have dropped some material called chaff from its airplanes. Chaff is an aluminum-fiberglass material, almost comparable
to Christmas tinsel, and is dropped from aircraft to confuse enemy radar.

After making several calls to see what operations the Navy may
have had ongoing at the time, and possibly involving chaff, I came
away with a series of "no's," "don't know of anything," and so forth.
Accordingly, I was quoted as disputing assertions made by San Diego
Gas and Electric Company (SDG&E) officials that the Navy was responsible for the problem.[9]

I reported this to my boss at the time, Vice Adm Crawford "Pete"
Easterling. Easterling was as rock-solid as they came—a no-nonsense
officer who did not suffer fools. I respected his leadership style, discipline, and focus and enjoyed working for him. Although he was responsible for all naval aviation matters in the entire Pacific Fleet
(including six aircraft carriers and hundreds of Navy tactical aircraft),
he was also the senior naval officer in San Diego. That responsibility
came with maintaining good relations with the media and community.

Easterling accepted the information we were given regarding the dropping of chaff—until a second power outage occurred six days later. This time, workers from SDG&E found tinsel-like material on a power station near Miramar Naval Air Station just north of San Diego. When I once again made calls to check on whether the Navy was using chaff on this occasion, I received similar responses—which equated to shoulder shrugs.

I remember standing before Admiral Easterling in his office the next morning after the second power outage—reading news reports that SDG&E personnel had found chaff-like material near a power facility. I remember him calling the commanding officer of the Miramar air station and ordering him (and a specific part of his rear body) to come over to his office on Coronado. About 20 minutes later, I looked out the admiral's office window and a Navy car arrived with three officers. When they entered Easterling's office, they were not greeted warmly. Instead, Easterling pointed at them and said something along these lines: "Do you know what you've made him do [pointing at me]? You've caused him to lie to the San Diego community and the media. Don't you ever put anyone in such a position again! If we made a mistake, fess up to it. You should be ashamed of yourselves." There were some strong expletives thrown in too. Nevertheless, the point was made, and I am sure the performance evaluations of the officers involved were appropriately annotated.

What made matters worse and what made me angry was the fact that the second outage was caused by some chaff accidentally falling from the aircraft upon takeoff from Miramar. When the chaff fell out of the plane, it landed on a nearby power station that sat near the end of the runway. I can only assume that Navy staff members were aware of the chaff that was accidentally discharged as soon as it happened. However, they chose to ignore it, hoping that the problem would go away.

I was embarrassed—not for those officers—but in my role as a naval officer. It was a huge black eye for the Navy and our standing in the community. I am sure my credibility with the local media was impacted too. However, at this point, it was not about me. As I stood watching and listening to Easterling chastise several senior officers, I sadly felt a sense of satisfaction. Nevertheless, when I looked at them, I could not believe they lied to me, which in turn led to my relaying false information to the community. I felt betrayed by fellow officers. This was not what the "book" said about officers possessing honesty and integrity. After conducting our investigation into the events, the Navy paid SDG&E nearly $50,000 for damages to its equipment.[10]

The Takeaway

If you are a leader, especially one that is in charge of an organization, act with integrity. Have the courage to make the right decision—not the easy decision. Be accountable to those you represent—whether it is a government department, agency, military service, trade association, corporation, or any other entity. You owe it to the taxpayer, shareholder, or whomever your stakeholders may be. Think about your actions. Do not be driven by politics.

Remember, especially those of you in government—whether you are a political appointee or a career public servant—you have a responsibility to the taxpayer. They pay your salary, and they also have a right to know what you are doing and why. To try to hide behind general information which is not even close to being sensitive or classified and sit on it is a nonstarter.

Political appointees, especially, need to be calibrated when they assume office. They are entrusted with supporting the Constitution—not the politician that gave them a job. Career public servants need to learn to think in the same vein. The public has a right to know.

And then there is the *lie*. There is nothing worse than telling a lie. It damages the soul of an organization and the people who represent it. As I stated earlier, once an individual tells a lie, his credibility is lost for a long, long time. Recovering from lying may never be possible. Moreover, this is as germane to a corporate or nonprofit entity as it is to a government agency. On a personal note, when I was a young boy, one of the things that my parents despised and were insistent on disciplining me for was for lying. Their lectures—and their resultant disciplining—have stayed with me to this day.

Notes

1. In simple terms, numismatic products are collector-quality coins.
2. Wikipedia, "Loonie."
3. Wikipedia, "Sacagawea Dollar."
4. The White House, "Campaign to Cut Waste."
5. The Dollar Coin Alliance, "Facts About the Dollar Coin."

6. The Dollar Coin Alliance, "Facts About the Dollar Coin."
7. John Adams to Thomas Jefferson, letter.
8. Lanzer et al., "The Science of Fake News."
9. Freed, "Navy Denies Being Cause of Blackout."
10. Weintraub, "Navy to Pay SDG&E; for Chaff Damage."

Chapter 5

The US Naval Academy

My Worst Fears Coming Home to Roost . . .
Media Access Was the Antidote

In 1994 the US Naval Academy was still reeling from a major cheating scandal that occurred in 1992 involving more than 125 midshipmen (students).[1] The Naval Academy was found to have serious deficiencies in how it conducted its investigation, so the Navy asked the Navy's IG to step in and do another investigation. The resulting report was rather strident and a "kick in the gut" as it said the Academy's honor code was flawed. The investigation found that 133 midshipmen had obtained advance copies of an exam and only 81 students admitted they cheated. However, most of them admitted to "repeatedly" lying during the first investigation conducted by the Naval Academy.

Richard L. Armitage, a former US ambassador, assistant secretary of defense, and a Naval Academy graduate, told the *Washington Post* that the IG report demonstrated that the tradition of honor at the Academy had been placed on the "back burner."[2] Armitage was a member of the Academy's board of visitors, an oversight board, and chaired a subcommittee that reviewed the school's honor code that states midshipmen "do not lie, cheat, or steal."

The cheating scandal garnered a significant amount of media attention, not just domestically but internationally, primarily because of the school's excellent global reputation of producing proud and polished naval officers. The scandal, unfortunately, occurred a few years after another incident that also received significant media attention. That incident was the chaining of a woman to a urinal in a male bathroom at the Academy.[3]

The Naval Academy needed new leadership to make a much-needed course correction and restore its image. Leadership was askew—along with a deviation from its moral compass. The answer was a four-star admiral, Adm Charles R. Larson—a very respected leader with impeccable credentials.

Previously, as Commander in Chief of the Pacific Command, Admiral Larson led 350,000 military personnel—Army, Navy, Air Force, and Marines—in the vast Pacific theater which spanned 40 countries.

Pres. William Clinton was impressed with Larson's leadership and considered him a strong contender to succeed Gen Colin Powell as chairman of the JCS. A White House fellow under Pres. Lyndon Johnson, Larson also served as a naval aide to Pres. Richard Nixon. He also commanded a nuclear submarine that completed some stunning missions off the coast of the Soviet Union during the Cold War. Despite all his impressive "tickets," Larson lost out to Army Gen John Shalikashvili to be chairman of the JCS and at that time, chose to retire.

Navy leadership saw an opportunity with Larson. Why let him retire? Instead, why not bring him back as a retired four-star and lead the Academy out of its malaise? Larson had previously served as superintendent of the Academy as a two-star admiral from 1983 to 1986, and the staff and faculty had a deep respect for him. When offered the opportunity to return to the school and provide a course correction for the school he graduated from and loved, Larson agreed.

However, his agreement to return came with some bargaining chips. One of the biggest ones was that he would not accept any Washington interference in the Academy for at least a year. With the Naval Academy in Annapolis, Maryland—so close to Washington and the Pentagon (36 miles)—Navy leadership seemed to have a penchant for getting involved in issues at the school. Larson wanted both civilian and military leaders to keep their "noses out of the tent." The Academy was also in the media spotlight, being so close to both Washington and Baltimore, two good-sized media markets. The media coverage of the urinal chaining and the cheating scandal was proof positive of such media frenzy.

When he assumed command of the school in 1994, one of the first things he did was meet with the faculty. Entering the room, before even uttering a word, Larson was greeted with a standing ovation. The greeting was an indication of just how much the faculty wanted Larson's leadership. Their hero had returned.

I was with Larson in Hawaii, at the rank of captain, when he asked me to join him at the Academy. He offered me the opportunity to return with him and be a part of his team. I welcomed the opportunity because there was undoubtedly much work to do in restoring the image of the school. I must admit that I was a bit concerned because I was not an Academy graduate. I was not sure if my lack of a "pedigree" would hurt my credibility. However, such butterflies quickly gave way upon arrival in Annapolis and the realization that having a "Larson pedigree" would more than suffice.

Having served at the school previously and witnessing what had happened in the subsequent years, Larson knew precisely the action to take. An adjustment or settling-in period was not necessary. He had to "hit the ground running," and he did so by establishing a new ethics and character development curriculum. He also tightened discipline—when midshipmen were allowed to leave campus, when they could wear civilian clothes, and when they could have a car. He also made changes that gave enforcement of the honor code "more teeth." He wanted to remind the midshipmen, along with the faculty and staff, that the Naval Academy was a military school. People came there because they wanted and expected discipline and leadership.

Larson's big focus was on ethics. Midshipmen were now required to read Plato and Aristotle and to visit the National Holocaust Memorial in Washington. Midshipmen formerly viewed leadership classes as "a joke," so they were restructured to ensure that integrity was the focus—not mere management techniques. Case studies in ethics were the norm for classroom discussions and essay responses replaced multiple choice and true/false quizzes. Larson even ensured that he attended some of the ethics classes and shared his own experiences with students.

For the first year, things went along swimmingly. Calm was the order of the day. Larson, being very civic-minded, was actively visible in the community—visiting and speaking with civic groups where he outlined his vision for the school and how he was putting it on the right course. He was very open with the media. We did one-on-one interviews and editorial boards with the *Capital* (the local Annapolis paper) and the *Baltimore Sun*. Larson also took the opportunity to visit with alumni and parent groups around the country. He preached the same message and outlined his corrective actions to steady the school. He was welcomed very warmly wherever he went.

Then the "roof fell in," and we were jolted back to reality. Staff and faculty were painfully reminded that the 4,000 students at the school were in many respects just like other college students. In the fall of 1995, two-dozen midshipmen were implicated in using or selling marijuana and the hallucinogenic drug LSD. Five midshipmen were suspected of felony drug distribution, and it was thought 19 midshipmen possessed enough for personal use. When I received the news on a Saturday evening, 14 October 1995, I felt like we had been "kicked in the gut." Things at the Academy had been turning around.

Other than having a horrific football team at the time, things were going well.[4]

When Larson learned of the issue, he immediately gathered his staff on Sunday afternoon to discuss our response to the matter. After staff members offered their recommendations, Larson informed us what he was going to do—give each member of the brigade (all 4,000 students) a urinalysis test.

I remember all staff members were quite surprised at the admiral's approach. I asked him what we were going to do if we had a large number of positives after giving the tests. His response was quite simple—we give the midshipmen due process, and if they are found guilty of drug use, we remove them from the Academy. Larson once again reminded his staff that we were a military school, and if all 4,000 members of the brigade tested positive, there were 4,000 more young men and women who would be more than delighted to take their places as members of the Naval Academy. Being a student here was a privilege and honor—not a right. Larson also reminded us that we had an obligation to American taxpayers who were then paying approximately $250,000 for each midshipman's four-year education.

The urinalysis testing began that Sunday evening. Interestingly, there were not enough urinalysis cups at the Academy—only enough for about half the brigade to get tested. Larson ordered more cups, and tested the remaining students the next day. The staff waited anxiously for the results, and when they arrived, we were both shocked and relieved. Of the approximately 4,000 midshipmen tested, none tested positive.

James Webb—a former senator from Virginia, secretary of the Navy in the late '80s, and 1968 Naval Academy graduate—lauded Larson for his bold initiative. In an opinion piece in the *Washington Post*, Webb said that the media were "flabbergasted" at Larson's willingness to test every midshipman. Nevertheless, Webb said that Larson believed in his people (the midshipmen) and they did not let him down. "Admiral Larson bet the brigade—and bet on the brigade, going all in—and won. At Tailhook '91, a long succession of high-rankers bet against the traditions and the respect of the Naval service and everyone lost," said Webb.[5]

Unfortunately, after a year of calm, the drug issue was the beginning of a series of other incidents that occurred in 1996—each one attracting national media attention. These incidents included the discovery of a car theft ring, a midshipman's involvement in child molestation, and the arrest of two drunk midshipmen for breaking into a home of one of the midshipmen's girlfriend. The problem with the latter incident was that the home the midshipmen were breaking into was the residence of the Maryland State Police superintendent. The incidents, when combined with the others that took place in the previous years, caused many to start asking the question, "What is wrong with the Naval Academy?"

Interestingly, it was the home break-in that caused a media onslaught. Media from both Washington and Baltimore came to Annapolis to interview Larson. There was a line of reporters waiting to speak with him. Larson and I discussed having a news conference to talk about the various incidents and our reactions to them. However, I felt a news conference would turn out to be analogous to a shooting gallery with Admiral Larson as the only target. A better alternative would be for Larson to do as many one-on-one interviews as possible. As mentally challenging and tiring as that would be, we would fare much better. Larson was calm under pressure and knew how to keep his emotions in check. He did a great job discussing his character development program and his other efforts to return the Academy to being a military school.

I also did several interviews with some of the media—smaller news outlets with reporters who were not as familiar with the school. They were not all that pleased with talking to a Navy captain when other competitors were talking to the four-star admiral. Either way, we gave them a "talking head," provided them access, and were responsive to their needs.

The entire situation, though, led to the *Baltimore Sun* assigning three of its most hardened and toughest reporters to follow the Academy full time. The *Washington Post* already had a reporter based in Annapolis full time covering state issues, but this reporter was now devoting the majority of her time to Academy issues. The local paper, the *Capital*, also had a reporter assigned full time to the Academy.

Larson was clearly under much pressure to do something. His ultimatum of one year without involvement from Washington was up, and Washington was putting together a blue-ribbon panel to "put its nose under the tent" at the Naval Academy.

At that point, Larson had enough and ordered something akin to a safety stand-down. As described in the introduction, when the military experiences a rash of safety-related accidents, a commander will frequently order a stoppage of all operations—or a "safety stand-down."

The stoppage—a day or a couple of days—is used to review procedures to ensure all the rules and policies are being followed. Larson wanted to do the same in the Academy's case. He wanted leadership—both at the staff and student level—to lead discussions about the Naval Academy culture and to drill down to what being a midshipman and a future naval officer meant.

The stand-down was productive, and Larson was extremely hopeful from what he saw and heard from the midshipmen leadership that was going to lead the brigade in the 1996–97 school year. At the same time, the 1996, or graduating class of midshipmen leadership, threw their hands up and said, "We're graduating in about a month, and we just want out of here." However, it was the rising seniors or first-class midshipmen that said they saw what Larson was trying to accomplish with his ethics, character development, and leadership program. They wanted to make some changes and wanted to lead by example. That is what Larson wanted to hear.

I had a strategy to get the media to understand what the Naval Academy was all about—developing future leaders. One of the ways I could do that was to provide them access to Bancroft Hall. Bancroft Hall is the largest college dormitory in the United States—probably in the world. It is where the midshipmen eat, sleep, and live. It is also where the Academy conducts much of its leadership development.

The problem I faced was that the media had never been allowed in Bancroft Hall. It was clearly "off-limits," and I wanted to break that barrier. The argument was that it was the midshipmen's home and access to it was inappropriate. I knew that arguing to allow media access was going to be difficult. "We haven't allowed media in there in 150 years, so why should we allow them now?" was a standard response.

The real reason for the trepidation was that sometimes there were some raised voices heard in Bancroft—perhaps some of the "in your face" variety of leadership that is, like it or not, part of the military culture.

Larson felt the Naval Academy was a leadership laboratory. During their four years at the Academy, midshipmen could observe, develop, and practice their leadership techniques and style. A good portion of those techniques could be learned and practiced in Bancroft. My argument to Larson about providing media access to Bancroft was that this is what made the Naval Academy different from every other civilian institution. Let us put our untoward incidents in the rearview mirror and showcase what we were really all about—developing leaders.

Of course, I received pushback from some of the old guard—those who wanted to do things the same way as they had been done in the past. However, I was able to get Larson to agree with me and to see the value of permitting media access to Bancroft Hall. At the time, I did not know how significant that access would prove to be.

In the near term, the dividends were significant. We allowed both the *Baltimore Sun* and *Washington Post* reporters (along with photographers) to observe what happens in Bancroft. They followed midshipmen around as they completed their daily routines. What resulted were some fantastic photo essays that seemed to make everyone quite happy. What had been mistrusted just a few weeks prior was suddenly labeled "great PR [public relations]" by formerly cynical Academy staffers. The *Baltimore Sun* did a "double truck" feature—two full pages that run on the adjoining left and right sides of the paper—on a set of twins from the Baltimore area that were graduating that spring.

Getting the class of 1996 graduated allowed everyone to take a deep breath. However, our reprieve was short-lived because it was only a few short weeks before the next class of plebes (freshmen) was to arrive in early July. Summers in Annapolis, like those in the entire mid-Atlantic region, are sweltering and humid. At the time, Bancroft Hall was not air-conditioned, so we took special care to ensure that we did not expose the young midshipmen to heat exhaustion.

Despite well-intended efforts, on a hot and humid Sunday afternoon in late July, I received a phone call from the duty officer in Bancroft Hall. I remember the phone call going something like this: "Captain, we had a situation here in the Hall that I wanted to inform you about. Everything is okay now, but we had some plebes who were being exercised [push-ups, jumping jacks, squat thrusts, and so forth] by a second class [junior] on the 4th deck. A couple of them passed out, but they were taken to the clinic, and they are now back with their company. They are all okay at this time. A first-class midshipman [senior] saw what was happening, and he jumped in and stopped the calisthenics immediately."

I thanked the young officer for the information, hung up the phone, and hung my head in dismay. I told myself that we had a very serious problem on our hands. The Naval Academy could withstand car theft. We could withstand a small cadre of midshipmen who were dealing in drugs. We could deal with a group of midshipmen cheating on an exam, and we certainly could withstand a drunken midshipman who would get caught breaking into his girlfriend's home. However, physical abuse of a trainee—another human being—was something that could not be tolerated. Amid all the issues that we were dealing with, there were several calls from members of Congress and others who were asking why we even needed service academies. They were expensive, and it was often asked, "Why do we need to spend so much money (approximately $250,000 in the mid-'90s) to train future officers when we could grow them in Reserve Officer Training Corps (ROTC) or Officer Candidate School (OCS) programs?"

I mentioned to my wife that if this incident ever got out—and I assured her that it would—I could see Admiral Larson being asked to testify before a congressional committee about midshipmen abuse. I went to work Monday morning fully expecting to receive a phone call from one of the media outlets covering us. The morning went by, and I felt a bit easier about it. Then when the phone rang shortly after lunch, it was one of the three *Baltimore Sun* reporters. He informed me that he had heard about the incident in Bancroft Hall the day before and asked me to comment on the matter. I told him exactly what happened and how a first-class or senior midshipman, using good judgment and leadership, stepped in to stop the calisthenics. I informed the reporter that the plebes were treated for heat exhaustion, were rehydrated, and returned to their companies. I also informed him that the second class midshipman was relieved of his duties and adequately disciplined.

The *Sun* reporter thanked me for the information and informed me that he would not be doing a story on the incident. He attributed his decision to the access that we had provided him and his team. They were able to witness the leadership we were trying to develop in Bancroft Hall, and that they believed the Sunday afternoon incident was an excellent example of what we were trying to accomplish. In this case, it was stepping in when you saw something occurring that you knew was wrong.

I breathed a sigh of relief . . . until I received a second call—this one from the *Washington Post* reporter. She relayed the same account of the incident and had all the details correct. When I told her what had happened, what actions occurred, and that the second class midshipman was relieved of his duties and disciplined, she responded in much the same way as her *Baltimore Sun* colleague—she decided there was not a story. She attributed her decision to the level of access provided to her and the leadership she witnessed in Bancroft Hall.

We had dodged a bullet—more like a rocket-propelled grenade. There is not a doubt in my mind that providing access to the media had saved us from further scrutiny.

Convincing leadership about the importance of providing access is not always natural. Sometimes it may appear to be easier to "fold up your tent" and move on to the next issue, but there are occasions when standing your ground and arguing for what you know is the right thing to do is essential. It may pay dividends.

The Takeaway

The value of providing access to the media was obvious, as was successfully demonstrated at the Naval Academy. While such a payoff may not be immediate, it is often like putting money in the bank of credibility and earning dividends for use at a later time. Be confident in the product and your people—or whatever you are trying to showcase. If that confidence is not there, then there is a leadership problem.

Engage the media regularly—not just when you need them. It is often too late when a problem or crisis arises. Let the media get to know you and your organization's leadership personally. Share your organization's vision, goals, and product(s). Make sure they have your phone number, and most importantly, answer your phone when reporters call you at any time of the day or night. Your media contacts do not have to become your best friends but consider them your *professional friends*. An occasional lunch or coffee is strongly recommended. An editorial board meeting with the head of the company or organization is also a consideration. Meetings like this send a powerful, cooperative, "We want to work with you" type of message.

Notes

1. Schmitt, "An Inquiry Finds 125 Cheated on a Naval Academy Exam."
2. Shen, "Probe Finds Extensive Coverup of Cheating at Naval Academy."
3. Barringer, "Harassment of Woman Shakes Naval Academy," and "Midshipman Leaves Naval Academy after Classmates Tie Her to Urinal."
4. Antonelli, "Naval Academy Tests for Drugs Action Taken in Wake of Arrest of Two Midshipmen."
5. Webb, "The Navy Adrift."

Chapter 6

A Murderer in Our Midst

How Leadership by Example and a Powerful Ethics Program Helped a Murderer Admit to Her Crime[1]

In the summer of 1996, a new class of plebes reported "aboard" the Naval Academy. The entire Academy staff was catching its breath after a tumultuous year of seemingly never-ending adverse events. The 1996–97 academic year had to be better.

In early September, I went to Massachusetts for the Labor Day weekend to be with my mother. My dad died the previous year, and my mother had a memorial service for him. Because of all that had happened the previous year at the Naval Academy, my mother was worried I would not be able to attend the service, but I assured her I would be there, and I was.

When I returned to Annapolis, we had our daily morning staff meeting with Admiral Larson on Tuesday, after the holiday. At the meeting, Larson said he wanted to see me, Joe (Capt Joe Scranton, the legal staff officer), and Hank (Capt Hank Sanford, Larson's executive assistant) after the meeting. The three of us meeting with the admiral was usually not a good sign—something was up.

Larson turned to me and said, "Tom, while you were gone, we had three things happen over the weekend. I just want to bring you up to speed." Scranton and Sanford were in Annapolis over the Labor Day weekend and were aware of what Larson was going to tell me. "The first incident involved a male and a female midshipmen who were in Georgetown [Washington, DC] over the weekend. The female is alleging that she was raped, and I just want you to be aware of the allegation," Larson said.

I responded that I appreciated the heads up and said I was sure the incident "no doubt" involved alcohol. About 85 percent of all disciplinary incidents involving midshipmen at the Academy were alcohol-related. Larson went on to inform me of a second incident—this one involving a staff chaplain. The chaplain was caught on a surveillance camera exposing himself to a young girl in an Annapolis department store. I remember being caught off-guard by that one and asked if the Annapolis police had booked the chaplain. He was booked, and therefore, there was an entry on the local police blotter. The incident was sure to attract media attention.

I told Larson that I saw an upward trend in the issues he was reporting. So what is the third issue, I asked?

"Well, I think we may have a murderer in the plebe class," he said.

In total disbelief, I remember my response: "Admiral, you have to be [actual expletive deleted] kidding me!"

"No. I wish I were, Tom."

How the Naval Academy helped solve the crime was fascinating— and a tribute to the ethics and leadership program that Admiral Larson had put in place upon his return to the Academy.

When Larson arrived at the school for his second tour, he knew what he needed to do to turn the school around and restore it to what it was. A lack of discipline was most evident. After all, it was a military school where order and discipline were mandatory. Accordingly, Larson led an effort to establish a leadership and character development program.

He also wanted to establish a significant and substantive ethics program at the school—not just a program that fulfilled a requirement by a bunch of boring lectures and some easy to pass true/false quizzes. He wanted a program put in place that made the midshipmen think about issues. Not all situations that midshipmen were going to face in the fleet as officers were black and white. Many were in the gray area, and not all were answered definitively. There certainly was not a shortage of ethical case studies for discussion.

What made Larson a great leader was his ability to analyze issues to the fullest and think through all possibilities. His ethics program was a perfect example and was imperative to him. Again, ethics and honor are a crucible for any officer and were an essential requirement for any leader; yet, he felt the honor concept at the Naval Academy had fallen by the wayside. A course correction was desperately needed.

Larson realized that if an ethics program was to be truly meaningful, the midshipmen were going to have to buy into it, believe it, and live it 24 hours a day. They must not only take ownership of it but also help enforce it. An effective ethics program cannot be an officer-to-a-midshipmen entity; it must be owned by the midshipmen and work simultaneously in both directions.

Larson met with the midshipmen honor committee, a group of upperclassmen, and explained that he wanted them to take ownership and responsibility and work with the whole brigade. In talking with the honor committee, the committee members told Larson that a "we versus them" or a "cops and robbers" mentality had been created at the school. If someone had done something wrong at the school, it was up to the administration or the active duty staff (the cops) to find out the violators of the rules (the midshipmen).

There was, in essence, tolerance for others doing wrong and being allowed to get away with things—just so long as you did not get caught. Before Larson's arrival, there was not a sense of an obligation to speak up if they saw something that was inappropriate or wrong. The best example was the cheating scandal. Many midshipmen knew what was happening and were a part of the problem, but they did not feel an obligation to speak up and enforce the honor concept. To many, the appropriate action was to turn their backs and walk away rather than uphold standards or enforce honor. The Academy honor concept had turned into a "hear no evil, see no evil, speak no evil" concept. This is what the Navy had seen demonstrated at Tailhook.

Put in place in 1995, Larson's character development and leadership programs began to take shape and catch on with the faculty, staff, and most importantly, the midshipmen. The proof of the midshipmen "getting it" came in the plebe class of the summer of 1996.

Plebes have very little free time during their summer training. What little time they do have comes during the evening hours before taps (in bed with lights out). During these short periods in the evening, the midshipmen would get to know each other a bit more and further their bonding. In 1996, during these evening discussions, one of the female plebes, Diane Zamora, kept asking her fellow female classmates what the worst thing they had ever done in their lives was. I imagine it was her version of truth or dare. Her classmates would answer with relatively simple examples—drinking underage, sneaking out of the house late at night to be with a boyfriend, and so forth.

When her classmates would turn the question around and ask Zamora, she would tell them that she had committed murder when she was in high school in Texas. Her classmates were in disbelief and thought her comments were just bluster. How could anyone admitted to the US Naval Academy have ever committed murder?

The discussions continued for several evenings, and Zamora's comments always came back to her committing murder in high school. Finally, Zamora's classmates had heard enough and felt it was time to inform their chain of command what they were hearing from her. Her classmates were convinced there might be something to her flamboyant talk.

After the plebes reported Zamora's comments to their midshipmen leadership (sophomores, juniors, and seniors), the upperclassmen in turn reported the comments to active duty staff members in their chain of command. To ensure Zamora's claims to the plebes were thoroughly investigated, one of the Academy's lawyers started calling various jurisdictions in Texas (Zamora's home state) to inquire about any unsolved murder cases. After numerous calls, they hit pay dirt.

One of the jurisdictions contacted by an Academy lawyer was Grand Prairie, Texas. When detectives acknowledged they did have an unsolved murder on their books and were told what was happening at the Academy, they quickly arrived in Annapolis. After questioning Zamora and her classmates, there was not a doubt in the minds of the detectives that Zamora had committed the crime. They also believed from questioning her that her boyfriend, David Graham, played a role in the murder. He happened to be a freshman at the Air Force Academy in Colorado Springs, Colorado.[2]

The detectives convinced the Naval Academy leadership to let Zamora go home for a few days on the guise of merely allowing her to take a deep breath after a very demanding summer of training. Detectives thought that Zamora and Graham, sensing the police were onto them, would collaborate on their stories. The detectives predicted that instead of going home to see her parents, she would arrive at the Dallas/Fort Worth International Airport and immediately take a flight to Colorado Springs to see Graham so they could get their stories in line. That is the course of action Zamora pursued.

The two were arrested and then tried and convicted of murder. The murder occurred in December 1995, only seven months before Zamora's arrival at the Naval Academy. The murder resulted from a lover's triangle. Zamora believed that a high school classmate, Adrianne Jones, was a romantic rival for Graham's affections. One morning in December, Graham used Zamora's car to pick up Jones. Zamora hid in the car's hatchback. They drove to a remote location where a struggle ensued. Zamora hit Jones over the head, and Graham shot Jones after she had broken away from Zamora.

The case received national media attention. The case provided *Court TV* with some of its highest ratings when it covered the trial.

Authors penned several books about the case and several made for TV movies featured the murder.

I have never liked the use of the term *spin* to describe working with the media. To me, spin has a negative connotation—twisting facts or embellishing the truth. Nevertheless, there was not a doubt in my mind, or the minds of any of us in leadership positions at the Academy, that the character development or honor program that Admiral Larson had put in place was the impetus that caused Zamora to come clean. The murder occurred in December 1995, and it was not until August 1996, after eight weeks of training—including a good dose of her first ethics training—that Zamora started to discuss her role in the death of her high school classmate. I used every opportunity I could to make this fact known.

Spin? I guess you could call it that, but I will stand by my belief to the day I leave this earth that Zamora's confession was the result of the ethics training she underwent during her summer in Annapolis. One of the themes of that training is *always* to do the right thing.

Some would argue that we were "making a silk purse out of a sow's ear." However, it was hard to argue against the role that the character development program played in solving this murder. The Grand Prairie Police Department and Adrianne Jones's family were very grateful.

The Takeaway

Good, sound leadership, as well as media access, can result in a big payoff. Admiral Larson and his willingness to cooperate with the media showcased his leadership and character development program. This level of cooperation—combined with his leadership style and willingness to interface with the student body and participate in ethics classes—sent a powerful signal, both internally and externally. To the media, it sent a strong message that Larson was adamant about turning around the image of the school. To the student body, it sent a similar message—that ethics and character were critical elements for naval officers.

Ultimately, as a result of the changing culture at the Academy, when Zamora told her classmates about her role in the murder of her high-school classmate Adrianne Jones, they felt comfortable in doing the right thing. Furthermore, the Academy's leadership and midshipmen's chain of command demonstrated they trusted the judgment of the classmates, and Zamora felt compelled to do the right thing by confessing to the murder.

When it became public knowledge that Zamora had been charged with murder, it was a very logical connection to make between the character development program and Zamora admitting to her crime. By showcasing the character development program well before the murder, when Zamora arrived at the school, it was easy to make the connection to the crime being solved.

I feel very strongly that if Larson had not recalibrated the Academy ethics program, the murder of Adrianne Jones would still be a secret between Zamora and Graham.

Notes

1. Sullam, "Some at Academy Did Right Thing in Murder."
2. Cardona, "What You Need to Know About the Teenage Love Triangle that Sent the Texas 'Cadet Killers' to Prison 20 Years Ago."

Chapter 7

The Importance of Being Responsive to the Media

In 2001, Lockheed Martin was awarded the contract for the most extensive military weapons system in history, the Joint Strike Fighter (JSF) or F-35 stealth fighter. When Lockheed announced the program, the plan was to buy more than 3,000 of the airplanes for a total program cost of more than $230 Billion. What made the program unique was that many of our nation's allies combined in joint task forces—hence the name *Joint* Strike Fighter—and agreed to participate in the program by contributing to the aircraft's manufacturing for their military's joint task force.[1]

The JSF was a highly visible program, visibility that continues today. As the program began to develop and unfold, there were the usual glitches that were expected with any new and complex program. By 2004, those glitches, or challenges, became apparent to both DOD and Lockheed. For example, as the detailed design progressed, weight estimates from an earlier design phase were found to be overly optimistic. Program leadership faced the fact that one of the airplane's variants would need to lose at least 3,000 pounds in order to meet performance requirements. Those working the program—at Lockheed Martin and the Pentagon—felt that a fix was either impossible or too expensive and time-consuming.

A team of 500 Lockheed Martin engineers miraculously fixed the problem and made other adjustments along the way. This included improving the structural integrity and making changes to the auxillary engine with a redesign that improved thrust. However, a redesign of this scope required restructuring the entire program plan, including a new schedule and additional program costs. "Free lunch" in the defense procurement business is a myth.

In early 2004, Lockheed established a new schedule and program cost for the program. Regardless, a Reuters defense industry reporter who followed the program closely somehow missed that the program had already been re-baselined (new cost estimates and schedule). When he learned of the new dates and schedule, he called Lockheed's Aeronautics business unit in Fort Worth, Texas.

Our communications and operational leadership staff in Fort Worth, unfortunately, did not respond quickly enough to the reporter's questions about a "new" schedule and program cost because of an ongoing senior staff meeting. In all fairness, I also think the Aeronautics staff thought the reporter had new information from the Pentagon or other sources that they did not have. Other problems with the JSF were finding their way into the program, such as new requirements and problems with the development of the 17 million lines of software code needed for the combat systems in the aircraft. Additionally, some of its capabilities were going to be deferred.

Unfortunately, the Reuters reporter filed a short, three-line story around 3:15 p.m. on 17 June 2004. Although the story was short, the lead sentence caught Wall Street's attention. It said Lockheed Martin was planning to delay the first planned flight of the JSF until 2006. Our stock opened trading that day at $49.40 a share and reached a high of $50.49, but as soon as the Reuters story hit the wires, the stock dropped precipitously—about $1.30 per share.

The lesson from this episode is how important it is to respond quickly to any reporter's requests for comment on significant programs—especially the programs that are the lifeblood of a company. A story like the one from Reuters can cause panic among investors, including institutional investors. For a joint program like the JSF, potential foreign buyers can also lose confidence in the program and its military and civilian leadership.

The Reuters reporter, frustrated by not receiving a quick response from our Aeronautics unit, should have dealt with his frustrations and had patience for a bit longer to ensure his story was accurate. Had he called my office before publishing his report, I may have been able to reason with him. In essence, there was fault on both sides.

Before the stock market opened the next day, we issued a press release explicitly citing the Reuters wire service story from the previous day. We said the story "mischaracterized a previously reported delay" in the JSF program. The release stated that schedule information reported in the "misleading" article had been previously reported several months prior. We also noted that the new schedule was reflected in our corporate earnings report released in April 2004.

Leaders at the Reuters newswire service were not pleased with our calling them out in our news release, but we felt it was necessary to set the record straight. It did have the desired impact as Lockheed Martin's stock opened on 18 June 2004, at $50.68—the bump resulting from our release.

The Takeaway

Being responsive to the press cannot be stressed enough. Letting things linger sends the wrong signal to the media that you are trying to hide something or come up with words that do not address the issue(s) at hand. Not being responsive can have a negative financial or reputational impact on an organization—and possibly both. A quick response to a given situation lessens that risk measurably.

Another lesson from this story is operational and manufacturing leaders should tell their PR staff members to interrupt them so that such news media queries can be addressed immediately—and to not wait until a routinely scheduled three-hour meeting is over. When that news query comes in via phone, email, or social media, the people responsible must respond. One of the worst things a company wants to see in print or hear on TV or radio is "a spokesman for the company did not respond before the deadline."

Notes

1. See "The Combined Joint Task Forces Concept."

Chapter 8

What to Do When the Media
Gets Under Your Skin

Don't Send Them to the Penalty Box, But Maybe
Give Them a Five-Yard Penalty

In September 2003, Lockheed Martin announced that it planned to acquire Titan Corporation for $1.8 billion in cash and stock. Lockheed Martin, the world's largest defense contractor, eyed Titan for its growing information technology business that included several contracts with US intelligence agencies, such as the National Security Agency. Titan employed about 11,000 employees, most of whom had security clearances in place. The large number of employees who had security clearances was a huge selling point since intelligence work was experiencing some exponential growth at the time, especially after 9/11, and it was costly for a company in both time and money to obtain security clearances for new employees.

The acquisition, however, did not come without baggage. Some Wall Street analysts felt Lockheed was paying too much for Titan. Another issue that arose once Lockheed began its due diligence after announcing the proposed acquisition was the rumor that Titan might have been engaging in bribery in an attempt to win overseas contracts—violations of the Foreign Corrupt Practices Act, which Congress passed into law in 1977. The law prohibits US firms and individuals from paying bribes to foreign officials in order to further a business deal.

As the vice president of media relations for Lockheed, I served as a spokesman for the company and defended our proposed acquisition. It was a huge acquisition, and the business media treated it accordingly. One of the outlets that covered the acquisition extensively was *Bloomberg News* and its reporter Ed Lococo. Some of the stories that Lococo had written on the planned purchase of Titan were not favorable, frequently quoting analysts who felt Lockheed was paying too much money for Titan. In the fall of 2003, Lococo filed a story on Lockheed Martin's JSF. This was a massive program for Lockheed because this multibillion program was one of the most significant contract wins for *any* defense contractor.

Robert Stevens, Lockheed's president and CEO, was in New York at a Wall Street analysts' meeting. Stevens was asked several questions about the JSF program at the meeting, and Lococo, listening to the conference on the phone, filed a story based on the comments Stevens made. The story, not the most positive, triggered an emotional response from Stevens. I knew it would when I sent it to him. As he was headed home from New York, he called me and said he was rather upset with Lococo's negative reporting on our new fighter.

Stevens asked me why we dealt with Lococo. He was referring to Lococo's coverage of the Titan acquisition and now a JSF story. He asked, "Why don't we simply shut him off?" I deflected the question and said we could talk more about it the next day after he returned to the office. I hoped that Stevens would calm down. He was always a very reasonable man and for the most part, very calm. I had never heard him this agitated, but I understood his emotions. On the Titan issue, many of the analysts were questioning Lockheed's judgment about the acquisition. Some analysts thought it was a prudent acquisition and the right fit for Lockheed. At the same time, the JSF program was in its infancy and was undergoing some natural growing pains.

The next morning my direct boss, Dennis Boxx, the senior vice president for communications, and I went to talk to Stevens about Lococo and *Bloomberg News*. Stevens was still upset. I was quite surprised that he was still "spun up" because my experiences with him had been that he usually "came down to Earth" pretty quickly. However, as we spoke, he began to return to his normal demeanor and asked us if we really thought we should terminate our relationship with Lococo—not *Bloomberg News*, just Lococo.

Unfortunately, both Boxx and I got caught up in the emotional aspects of Locco's article taking our company to task. We were both very loyal to Lockheed Martin, of course, and it stung to see Lococo quoting analysts who felt the Titan acquisition was not a prudent decision. Then, when you factor in Lococo's most recent story on the JSF, you could say, "enough was enough." We felt that since we were the "big dog on the block"—the world's largest defense contractor— we could call the shots. So instead of talking Stevens out of terminating our relationship with Lococo, we did it. The action was a big mistake.

I sent Lococo a letter, with a copy to his editor, informing him of our decision. We indicated that we would most welcome working with other *Bloomberg* reporters—but not Lococo. The *Bloomberg* leadership team was somewhat shocked at our decision, and some of their editors called immediately to see if we would reconsider. How could Lockheed Martin, the world's largest defense contractor, not want a relationship with a reporter from the world's premier business media outlet? Another *Bloomberg* reporter, Tony Capaccio, who covered the Pentagon beat and with whom I had successfully worked with for years, called me and said, "Do you guys know what you've just done? Are you serious?"

One month turned into two, then three. Over the next couple of months, *Bloomberg* editors from both Washington and New York came to Lockheed Martin's corporate headquarters in Bethesda, Maryland, to meet with Boxx and me. We stood our macho ground. Lococo, meanwhile, being the professional that he was, continued to call us every time he had a story for which he needed a Lockheed comment. On every occasion, we declined, reminding him of our policy decision not to work with him. Consequently, every *Bloomberg* story on Lockheed Martin carried the following sentence: "A Lockheed Martin spokesman declined to comment."

Finally, after about eight months, Boxx and I came to the same conclusion. It was time to let Lococo out of what we called the "penalty box" and start working with him again.

If I had to do it all over again, I would have been much more adamant about not going in the direction that we did and thought through our decision quite a bit more. In hindsight, there is not a doubt in my mind that I could have talked Stevens and Boxx into going in the opposite direction—and I should have. They were both extremely reasonable people, and it was a bad call and one that I would never make again. I was ruled by emotion, and that is never a good thing in our business. If I had heard of someone else making this same decision, I probably would have said, "You what? Why did you ever do that?"

The irony of this story is that Lockheed Martin pulled out of the Titan deal after Titan failed to reach a plea agreement with the Justice officials had bribed individuals in Saudi Arabia and Benin to win contracts. Titan wanted to extend the deadline for the plea agreement; however, when it became clear that the Justice Department investigation was continuing, Lockheed pulled out.

Lococo and *Bloomberg* probably had every right to say to Lockheed, "We told you so." Nevertheless, they did not. In retrospect, Lococo was an outstanding reporter—thorough and meticulous. He always asked appropriate questions and was intelligent. When I look back on my professional career and think about some of the mistakes I have made, this one ranks at the very top.

One thing to remember when reading or hearing about your organization is the importance of differentiating between a story you do not like and one that is incorrect. When you see an inaccurate report, call the reporter—do not email or text—and report that they have incorrect facts. Ask for a correction. Any reporter "worth their salt" will do so immediately. A reputable reporter does not want to be wrong and is committed to correcting errors of fact. It is in their DNA.

Reading or seeing a news report you do not like is a different story. Ask yourself the following questions:

- Is there a grain of truth to what is being reported?
- Was the situation being discussed in the story handled correctly?
- Is the customer who is complaining about the customer service he or she received justified in their comments?
- Is the community legitimately concerned about this issue?
- Have you responded appropriately and adequately to those concerns?
- Were your comments fully and accurately presented?

If your questions are not appropriately answered or have inaccurate information, you have reason to be upset and request clarification or an updated news report. However, if your organization did not adequately present its case, and you expected the community and the media to read your mind, you do not have anyone else to blame but yourself.

But Sometimes a Judgment Call May Be in Order

As the last decade of the twentieth century approached, it was clear to many that a new world order was forming. Pres. Ronald Reagan built positive relations with Soviet president Mikhail Gorbachev—they formed such a harmonious relationship that he urged Mr. Gorbachev to "tear down this wall." So when the Berlin Wall fell in 1989 after a series of uprisings in several Eastern Bloc countries, the physical wall coming down did not come as a surprise. Many credit Reagan's statement and his relationship with Gorbachev.

As I prepared to depart Washington in the spring of 1990, after a four-year assignment working for Admiral Trost, the CNO, I began to look ahead to my new assignment as a Navy captain working as the PA officer for the US Pacific Fleet at its headquarters in Pearl Harbor, Hawaii. There, I would be working for Adm Charles "Chuck" Larson. Before leaving for Pearl Harbor, I learned that two significant events had been approved and scheduled by the US and Soviet governments. One would be a visit by three Soviet Navy ships to San Diego in August 1990 and a reciprocal visit by three US ships to Vladivostok, Russia, a month later. The US Navy had not made a port visit to a Soviet or Russian port in 53 years. Times were definitely changing.

These events were going to attract much attention. The fact that the Soviet Union had invited me and other Navy staffers to its embassy in Washington before I departed for Hawaii to discuss plans for the events spoke volumes. A "working" visit to the Soviet embassy by a US Navy officer just a year before would have been unheard of—not to mention that three Soviet warships were coming to San Diego and three US Navy ships were visiting a Soviet Union port. We were warmly received and treated at the embassy, as both sides were anxiously looking forward to the port visits.

The Soviet Navy's visit to San Diego went well. However, it was marred on the last day. A US Navy female sailor alleged that she was assaulted and raped by a Soviet sailor while touring one of the Soviet ships earlier in the week. The female sailor went to a civilian rape crisis center in San Diego, and the center reported the event to the NIS—the precursor to what is now known as Naval Criminal Investigative Service (NCIS)—and the NIS investigators wanted to pursue the alleged criminal matter vigorously.

Admiral Larson, however, did not have faith in NIS, and neither did other Navy leaders at the time. NIS had an image of wanting to pursue any issue reported to it, regardless of the amount of evidence. Larson and his Soviet counterpart discussed the matter and exchanged information. After review, Larson did not feel there was sufficient evidence to pursue the matter. Accordingly, the Soviet ships departed San Diego as scheduled. The ensuing media coverage marred an otherwise diplomatically successful Soviet visit.

Several weeks later, Larson and I, along with some Pacific Fleet staff members and three news media representatives, were on board the guided-missile cruiser USS *Princeton* headed for Vladivostok. The three reporters were Greg Vistica with the *San Diego Union*,

Ed Offley with the *Seattle Post-Intelligencer*, and Neil Strassman with the *Long Beach Independent Press-Telegram*. One of the three ships scheduled to participate in the visit, USS *Blue Ridge*, did not sail to Vladivostok and instead was ordered to sail to the Persian Gulf after Saddam Hussein invaded Kuwait. USS *Princeton*, a guided-missile cruiser, and USS *Reuben James*, a fast frigate, participated in the visit.

The weeklong visit was one of the highlights of my 31-year career in the Navy. Just standing on the deck of USS *Princeton* and seeing the Cyrillic writing on signs as we pulled into Vladivostok—along with children waving American and Soviet flags—was a surreal experience. In the past, the Soviets were the *enemy*—the big, bad bear—and we were in its den. The Soviet Union was the country whose navy harassed us on the high seas with dangerous maneuvers. This was the country whose ships endangered my first ship, an aircraft carrier, by crossing its bow at 500 yards, a dangerous distance, when I was an ensign. They then blinded me and the rest of my watchstanders with a bright signal light shined at night into our bridge. Nevertheless, 20 years later, here we were.

The entire Vladivostok experience was incredible, but we were faced with another issue that had the potential to mar the entire event. While in Vladivostok, Vistica befriended a local college student and his girlfriend. Vistica had the couple take him to a town in Siberia called Gradekovo. Gradekovo was a small town about 150 miles northwest of Vladivostok and 10 miles east of the China-Russia border.

Visitica was a gifted reporter. As a congressional aide, a reporter for the *San Diego Union, Newsweek, 60 Minutes II, New York Times Magazine,* and the *Washington Post*, Vistica had a solid understanding of international affairs. When Vistica told the college couple where he wanted to go, he had expectations of what he would find, and those expectations were met.

What he saw was a large assemblage of Chinese and Soviet military forces on the Sino-Soviet border. Relations between China and the Soviet Union were frosty, at best, during this period. A conflict had erupted on the Chinese/Soviet border in 1969 that some predicted might have led to World War III. Just 10 years before that conflict, China and the Soviet Union were in lockstep as communist brethren. However, those ties began to erode over ideological, leadership, and resource differences. Those differences exacerbated territorial disputes that began in Tsarist and Imperial periods.[1] The tensions culminated in the 1969 clash between Chinese and Soviet forces.

When Vistica arrived at the border in 1990, tensions had eased, but military forces were still present. He took pictures of the forces that were massed and returned to USS *Princeton* where he wrote a story about what he had witnessed. Because communications were not as instantly transmittable as they are now, Vistica brought his news report to the communications department onboard the ship, where he requested that it be sent to his editors in San Diego.

When some very astute Navy communications technicians saw the story, they immediately notified their superiors, who then apprised Larson and me of the story's contents. Larson directed that the story not be transmitted—and I had to relay our decision to Vistica.

Larson was concerned that if the story was transmitted and appeared in the paper, the Soviets would be very upset. Larson reasoned that we were guests in their country, we were there as part of a diplomatic effort, and a story about Chinese forces being massed on the border would lead the Soviets to believe that Vistica was nothing more than a mere spy disguised as a reporter. The Chinese, on the other hand, would think we were spying for Russia.

Larson had superb skills as a warrior, as he demonstrated when he was a submariner during the Cold War. The tactics he demonstrated underwater were legendary but were mostly classified. He was also known as a skillful diplomat, and those are the skills he demonstrated when he did not allow the transmission of Vistica's story. Had the Vistica news report been sent to his editors in San Diego, I firmly believe that the entire port visit would have backfired from its intended diplomatic purpose—with the Soviets asking us to leave Vladivostok.

When he returned to the states, Vistica filed his story.[2] It was soon followed by a call from Jerry Warren, then editor of the *San Diego Union,* to me. Warren, who had previously served as a White House press secretary, proceeded to "tear into me" unlike any other admiral or senior officer had done—and some of the best had verbally ripped me. Warren proceeded to lecture me about how Vistica was a guest aboard the ship, that we had violated our commitment to him, and that we had violated the democratic principles of freedom of the press.

When I took the call, I had a feeling about what I could expect from the editor. I understood Warren had to stick up for his reporter. I would expect nothing less, but as naval officers—and as representatives of our government—we had an obligation to support the mission of establishing better relations between both countries. We were not asking Vistica to kill his story. We wanted the story held until he returned to the states. When Vistica did file his story, it carried the caveat that the Navy had refused to transmit the story over its communications system because of the potential impact on US-Soviet relations. From my point of view, I thought the caveat was accurate and quite fair.

If faced with a similar situation today, the question is, what would I do? The answer is, I do not know. So many situations in our business have to be evaluated on their merits, and often, situations are not necessarily black or white. They are often gray, and judgment calls have to be made. In the case of Vistica's visit to the border, you have to ask what the reaction might have been not only from the Soviets but also from the Chinese. Also, it was a different time in foreign relations history. The Cold War had just barely ended. Things were looking promising for putting some of our differences aside. So why put them in jeopardy over a story that could wait?

The truth of the matter is that Vistica or any other reporter faced with a similar situation today could easily file a story by merely placing it on his or her cell phone and pressing a button.

Interestingly, China and Russia signed a peace treaty in 1991, one year after the US Navy visit. The agreement resolved most of the border disputes between the two countries.

To further illustrate how the geopolitical situation between the two countries has changed, in 2018, Russia conducted its most massive military exercise in almost four decades, with more than 300,000 soldiers and 1,000 aircraft. The exercise included an invitation to China to participate. China accepted the invitation, and more than 3,000 Chinese soldiers took part.[3]

The Takeaway

Reporters can get under your skin. They have a job to do, and most of the reporters I have dealt with are committed to seeking balance in reporting their stories. To have balance requires engaging them and providing useful information. In the case of Lococo, perhaps we should have tried a bit harder and had him meet with our CFO or even our CEO, who could explain why Lockheed wanted to acquire Titan. Perhaps we could have repeated the process with the JSF issue—had him meet with a subject matter expert in our Aeronautics business unit and explain to him why the program was suffering cost growth rather than simply answering his questions.

As it turns out, of course, Lococo and those who were cautioning Lockheed about acquiring Titan were right.[4] However, it was not for the reasons they were articulating. As it turned out, Titan was alleged to have bribed some foreign governments to win contracts. On 2 March 2005, Titan admitted to illegally providing $2 million to the 2001 re-election campaign of Pres. Mathieu Kerekou of Benin. Titan pleaded guilty and paid the largest penalty under the Foreign Corrupt Practices Act in history for bribery and filing false tax returns. If the acquisition had been completed, and Titan found guilty, Lockheed Martin would have been liable for the fines.

The bottom line is to "suck it up" and learn to live with some of the more challenging members of the news media. Engage them. Work with them. Call them in and offer them an opportunity to interview an organizational leader. If it does not work, at least you know you tried.

There is an ancient saying in the communications business that pertains to print media. However, even in the digital age, it has significance and, in actuality, even more significance. The saying is, "Don't mess with an organization that buys ink by the barrel and paper by the ton." In today's environment, this could be expanded to include "an organization with an unlimited supply of digital pages and server space."

The Vistica episode is a bit different in that it demonstrates that often we are faced with situations that require judgment calls. Some situations we face are clearly black and white. On the other hand, others are gray without a right or wrong answer. You will most likely take "heat" for whatever direction you choose. The only thing you can count on is that you may be criticized for a decision, but you need to remain confident in your rationale and for going in the direction you chose.

Notes

1. Farley, "How the Soviet Union and China Almost Started World War III."
2. Vistica, "On the Frontier of Soviet-Chinese Relations," A2.
3. Grove, "Russia and China Plan Joint War Games," A18.
4. Wikipedia, "Titan Corporation."

Chapter 9

Leaning Forward and Taking Prudent Risks Can Pay Dividends

A recurring issue at Lockheed Martin was the inaccuracy of the press reports when we issued our quarterly earnings news releases at 7:30 a.m. every quarter. I thought I had a solution to the problem.

Because of our company's size—with more than 100,000 employees across the globe, revenues greater than $50 billion, and several business units and lines of business—our earnings press releases were long and packed with facts and figures. A ten-page release was not uncommon. The size of the releases and the amount of information contained in them reflected transparency and the commitment by leadership to full disclosure. Unfortunately, as well-intentioned as we tried to be, it created a few problems for us.

When we issued our earnings releases, we would put a small group of reporters—about five or six—on the phone individually for about five to seven minutes beginning at 7:35 am with our CFO. In essence, we would give reporters just a few minutes to digest a ten-page news release. Because of their haste, these reporters were forced to distribute a story about our performance, and many of them did not have an opportunity to absorb fully the information contained within the fact-filled release. As a result, stories frequently contained inaccurate information when they started crossing the newswires around 8 a.m.

At 11 a.m., it was our standard practice for the CEO and CFO to have a conference call with Wall Street analysts who covered the defense sector. Unfortunately, because of the misinformation or inaccuracies that resulted from the rushed news stories posted earlier that morning and already "on the street," the CEO and CFO would take precious time at the beginning of their call correcting those stories. That time could have been better spent talking about the company's vision and the many positive things we were doing.

After giving the issue considerable thought, I came up with a possible solution to the recurring problem—issue our press release to a selected group of reporters that covered the defense industry the evening before our earnings release. However, the understanding with them was that they would accept our release on an embargoed basis. The embargo would be lifted when our release went out the next morning at 7:30 a.m. This plan would give select reporters and their major news organizations time to absorb the material and ask questions during the calls that began at 7:35 a.m. before filing their stories. The hope was to minimize confusion and improve the accuracy of the information reported.

The biggest hurdle in executing this strategy was to convince our CEO and CFO that this new process was going to work and that each reporter whom we provided our release to was going to abide by the embargo. There was risk involved. The Securities and Exchange Commission (SEC) does not look kindly on companies that leak information that can affect a company's stock price or selectively provide that information to one group before another. It is frowned upon and can lead to severe fines and damage a company's reputation.

On the bright side, I was able to convince our CFO that if we were to provide our earnings release the evening before to a small group of *trusted* reporters that we would be helping ourselves in the end. The reporters I provided the release to clearly understood the situation and realized the ramifications of a busted embargo. Accordingly, they appreciated the trust we placed in them.

The result was that much more accurate and thoughtful reporting occurred and fewer diversions ensued on the 11 a.m. call with Wall Street analysts.

Joan Lunden and *Behind Closed Doors*

As the Navy started to work out of its funk resulting from multiple issues—the poor handling of the 1989 explosion on the battleship USS *Iowa*, the Tailhook '91 scandal, the various issues at the Naval Academy during the 1990's, and the 1996 suicide of the CNO (Adm Mike Boorda)—the Navy's leadership and the PA community realized we had much work to do to regain the trust of the American public. In truth, the Navy's image and reputation would have recovered on its own, given time. However, those of us who wore the uniform—and who knew we could do something to help turn the corner—could not stand by idly and wait for a self-correction. It was not part of the DNA of Navy PA officers.

To invite the news media to sea to witness our hardworking men and women and the sacrifices they make every day involved risk. What would happen if a media member met that one unhappy sailor? What would happen if an accident happened aboard one of our ships while the media were aboard? After all, we work in a dangerous environment, and we had to weigh the risks against the possible rewards. The answer was "yes"—the risk is certainly worth the reward. However, it must be undertaken thoughtfully and carefully, and that is what the Navy did. They thoughtfully and carefully invited a mixture of print, television, radio, and even emerging internet news outlets—both national and local—out to sea to witness and document the Navy's professional and hardworking sailors doing their jobs.

This enormous undertaking was skillfully initiated by my predecessor and the Navy's Chief of Information at the time, Rear Adm Kendell Pease. Pease set a pleasant tone and was aggressive, both tactically and strategically. Quite simply, he was not afraid to tell the Navy story. Because of Pease, the Navy enjoyed numerous PR successes both locally and nationally.

Joan Lunden, formerly a co-host of ABC-TV's *Good Morning America*, left the network to begin a series of her own called *Behind Closed Doors*. The show was a series of documentaries Lunden hosted and aired on ABC, along with the A&E Network. On both programs, Lunden was provided access to many organizations and locations where the public was not allowed. For example, the CIA, the FBI's hostage rescue team, and a women's maximum-security prison were some of the places she visited. Furthermore, the Navy wanted in to tell its story and Pease made that happen.

Accordingly, Lunden was invited to visit an aircraft carrier and ride in the backseat of an F/A-18 fighter. To fly aboard in a tactical aircraft would require her to undergo training. This rigorous training became part of her documentary. While preparing for her ride in a tactical aircraft, she was able to observe female Navy pilots on their way to becoming the first aviation combat-qualified women in the Navy. This was a perfect PR antidote to some of the issues resulting from the Tailhook '91 scandal. Her visit to the carrier USS *Eisenhower* was a total success and accomplished precisely what we wanted when we sent out our invitation.

She was also invited to go aboard a Navy nuclear submarine, USS *Key West*. Before embarking on the submarine, Lunden went to New London, Connecticut, where she observed submarine training and participated in some drills where she witnessed the dangers of flooding and fires aboard a submerged ship. She and her crew were able to capture the training submarine sailors go through and how professionally they respond to such situations.

While aboard *Key West,* Lunden participated in a combat exercise where a Navy SEAL team embarked on the submarine participated in a simulated combat exercise ashore. The mission for the SEAL team was to assess the damage to targets after a simulated Tomahawk cruise missile strike.

Lunden's visits to both the carrier and the submarine can be viewed on *YouTube.* A viewer will see and hear how the access that was provided to Lunden paid considerable dividends for the Navy and the American taxpayers. These visits greatly enhanced the Navy brand. However, enhancing the brand of any organization or entity begins with access, and sometimes it takes effort to convince the leadership of an organization that there will be a payoff.

NBC's *Today Show* and Matt Lauer

Another project that I became involved in was the *Today Show* and its co-host, Matt Lauer. In the late 1990s, the *Today Show* did a week-long set of segments entitled "Where in the World is Matt Lauer?" For five days that week, Lauer would turn up in various geographic locations across the globe.

In May 1999, in NBC's preparation for the various segments, I was approached by an executive producer for the *Today Show,* Susan Lasalla. She asked me if the Navy would be willing to do a two-hour live show from an aircraft carrier—one that was currently deployed overseas and preferably underway. I was serving as the Navy's chief of information at the time.

All sorts of thoughts ran through my mind. Initially, my reaction was, "Wow. What a great idea and opportunity." However, the more I thought about it, the more I began to run through all the negatives in my mind. For example, would technology support it? If you recall, satellite transmissions were not nearly as reliable then as they are now. How do we control whom Lauer interviews aboard the ship? Is he going to find that unhappy sailor aboard the ship? If that sailor is asked if he is comfortable with females aboard his ship, what is he going to say? In contrast, when Lauer speaks to a female sailor, what is she going to say about how accepted she is as part of the crew?

We looked at the schedule for our carriers for the selected week The *Today Show* and Lauer were planning. USS *Theodore Roosevelt* was scheduled to be in Antalya, Turkey. Assigned to the US Sixth Fleet, it would be getting prepared to get underway for a transit through the Bosphorus and back into the Mediterranean Sea. After getting a thumbs-up from Navy leadership, we told NBC it was a "go" and proceeded with the planning.

In a nutshell, the show was executed flawlessly and was a significant boost for morale throughout the entire Navy. Mechanically and technically, everything worked perfectly. From the content perspective, I can honestly say the same. The sailors—men and women of all ranks—were proud of the Navy and their jobs. They were just as articulate as the sailors aboard the submarine with Joan Lunden. Their stories were *the* stories of the Navy.

It was a home run. I will never forget a phone call I received at about 9:10 a.m. on the day the segment aired. Lauer had just bid his farewells from the aircraft carrier, and the New York crew closed out the show. Part of the mystique about the Lauer segments was that the New York crew did not know where Lauer was going to be on any given day during the "Where in the World" segments.

My aide came into the office and said I had a phone call that I needed to take. He would not tell me who it was, just that I should take the call. I thought it might be my wife who was calling to congratulate us on the show's success. When I picked up the call, the voice at the other end was Katie Couric, who was ecstatic. Before offering her congratulations, she asked one question: "How in the hell did you pull that one off?" I had worked with Couric when she was an assistant producer for NBC covering the Pentagon with then correspondent Jim Miklaszewski.

The visit would have never occurred without the approval for access from Navy leadership, and I would have never considered the project if I did not have faith and confidence in our equipment and the people who operate it. Those qualities and criteria are valid for any organization, be it a military unit, a corporate or private entity, a nonprofit organization, or a government agency.

Access—prudent access—can be "keys to the kingdom" if an organization wants its story told. You have to participate with the news media and grant them access if you hope to have fair news coverage.

The Takeaway

Sometimes, taking a risk is worth the reward. When given those opportunities or when thinking about something that you would like to do, sit down with your staff and talk about the risks, the rewards, and the possible pitfalls. Reach some form of consensus and proceed to make the "go/no-go" call.

Usually, if the decision comes down to one of access, lean in that direction. Ensure that you have all the ground rules in place and that the necessary players are briefed as to what goals you are trying to achieve. Prepping the players with reliable messaging is always a prudent action to take. It is a critical element of success. All sailors in the Navy and all employees of an organization need to understand what part they play in the big picture.

Recalling Gen Walt Boomer's words in *Proceedings* is most appropriate here:

> If you are going to do that [let the media interact with the sailors on a ship or employees in an organization], you better have faith in your troops. If you don't trust them, you can't turn the media loose. But I would submit that if you don't have faith and don't trust them, you're not a very good leader and you shouldn't be there either. You've got to be able to deal with the one percent that is going to say what you don't want them to say . . . Ride that storm out; don't shut it down because of the one percent.[1]

Notes

1. Boomer, "Stop Whining," 2.

Chapter 10

A Lawyer's Job Is to Provide Advice . . . But the CEO or Commander Is the Final Authority

One thing I learned early on in my career is the importance of depending on and trusting lawyers to give you good advice and direction. I always remember early in my career a Navy lawyer telling me, "Remember, if you are going down a certain path and it's illegal, we'll always tell you. Otherwise, if we provide you advice and recommend that you do such and such, you don't always have to take our advice. It's just that—advice."

I will always remember that, and I found that principle very accurate. Often, communicators and lawyers work in areas that are not always clear-cut. Those areas are frequently complicated, and a decision could be made to go in a variety of directions. It is also not unusual for lawyers and PA/PR staff members to have a different perspective on an issue. That difference could conceivably lead to significant consequences when both groups need to discuss the situation with the commanding officer or the company executive. He or she needs to know both sides of an issue—the pros and cons of making a decision—and it is helpful, and indeed more comforting, if the executive knows the lawyer and the PA/PR staffer are on the same page.

I was blessed to have worked with some tremendous lawyers in both the Navy and at Lockheed Martin. One of the lawyers at the US Mint, however, was not in that category. I will discuss him in a few moments.

My takeaway here is that it is crucial to have a good, sound professional relationship with your legal team. The lawyers do not have to be your best friends, but when you have a problem and you need advice, you can go to them and feel confident about what they are going to tell you. On the other hand, counsel needs to make *you* aware of any issue before the media calls you about it. Relationships with your legal team, just as they are with the media, are formed on trust; and you know you are on the team when the lawyers alert you to an issue.

For example, when Lockheed Martin began the purchase of another company (e.g., the purchase of Titan discussed in chapter eight), the lawyers called me in as soon as those discussions began. I immediately began to prepare myself with talking points and questions that I could anticipate from the media as well as prepared answers to those questions. I had daily discussions with the lawyers—they would keep me apprised as the discussions continued—right up until it was time to formally announce the intended purchase. For example, as the Wall Street analysts and financial and defense trade media began their dissection of the Titan purchase, the lawyers helped me.

Similarly, when I was at the Naval Academy, and we thought we had a murderess in the student body (discussed in chapter six), the lawyers kept me in the loop as the issue progressed. Admiral Larson, the superintendent, approved lawyers calling various jurisdictions in Texas to see if they had any unsolved murders on their books. For the same reasons I have discussed in chapter three regarding the mishandling of the Tailhook incident, he purposely did not call in the NCIS. Larson felt they would interject themselves into the matter and leak the situation to the media well before the matter was resolved. He did not trust NCIS, but he did trust the lawyers, and they kept us informed.

The many lawyers I have worked with—with one exception—had an excellent read on reality. I have found them to have a good understanding of the media, how it works, its importance in a democracy, and what its responsibilities are to our nation. It was refreshing, as I was frequently impressed with their perspective. This allowed them to be a great sounding board when I wanted to go in a particular direction. They would often say, "Well, if you say this, you better be prepared to answer that" or "If you do this, you are going to go down a dangerous path."

After healthy and positive relationships with countless lawyers, I arrived at the US Mint to meet a lawyer whose nickname was "Dr. No." He thrived on disapproving a variety of efforts to make the Mint a better place to work, sell numismatic products, and create more interest in coin collecting. The US Mint is a unique entity because it is one of the few government agencies that actually manufactures items—coins used for commerce or sold to individuals who wanted to purchase them as gifts. Many of the products manufactured and sold are made of gold and silver.

At the time of my tenure there, from 2009 to 2017, the Mint's leadership was desirous of advertising its products. After all, in some respects, it offered a retail operation that could return money to the Treasury's General Fund (and the taxpayer). However, the leadership at the US Treasury would not approve any advertising expenditures. For example, when I asked why we could not advertise in *Parade* magazine—when the Littleton Coin Company advertised our products every week and made a significant profit by marking those prices up—I was told, "Mr. Geithner [Treasury Secretary at the time] would choke on his Cheerios if he opened up *Parade* magazine on Sunday morning and saw an ad in there from the Mint."

I found it hard to believe that Geithner, after his experiences in the corporate world, would not approve an advertising budget. I believe to this day that he was unaware of the policy that others had made regarding advertising. What type of organization with a retail function fails to advertise?

I never forgot having dinner with a group of numismatists, coin dealers, and numismatic journalists at a massive coin show. A charming gentleman who was sitting across from me asked where I worked and what I did. After I informed him of my function—director of Corporate Communications at the US Mint—I asked about his profession. He smiled and said, "I'm Dave Sundman. I'm the president of Littleton Coin Company."

I told him I saw his ads, advertising our products in countless publications. He thanked me for recognizing his ads and asked why the US Mint did not advertise. I told him about the Treasury Department edict, and he quickly responded with a smile and added how that policy was fantastic for his business—a boon, if you will.

My point is that the lawyers at Treasury could have stepped in and enlightened Mr. Geithner and his deputy. This policy could have quickly been overturned, and the taxpayer would have been a beneficiary.

One additional example clearly illustrates the mindset of the US Mint lawyer and his "Dr. No" persona. It was my first year at the Mint, and employee morale was low—near the bottom of all federal agencies and bureaus. Federal agency and bureau employees are given surveys each year that measure morale, working conditions, and their opinions about the leadership they are provided. *Best Places to Work* (in the federal government) published the results in an annual listing. The survey and rankings are produced by the nonpartisan Partnership for Public Service and measure employee engagement government-wide, as well as at individual departments and agencies. The rankings provide a means of holding leaders accountable for the health of their organizations. The rankings spotlight agencies that successfully engage employees, as well as those that fall short.

I saw our low standing—201st— as a challenge.[1] As the communications director for the Mint, I had an opportunity to help raise it. I saw how hard our employees at our manufacturing facilities worked, and they deserved some recognition for the job they did—both internally and externally.

One of the initiatives we undertook was a "Bring Your Children to Work Day"—much like at numerous other federal agencies and private firms. At headquarters, we arranged a variety of activities for the kids. One parent who worked in our human resources department thought of a great idea—videotaping the kids doing a simulated TV commercial for a specific coin. We would tape each child doing a commercial and then play a composite of the "ads" on our internal Mint TV system. A consent form was provided to each parent, agreeing that we would be taping their child and stating that the segments would only be used internally.

When the lawyer heard about the idea, he immediately nixed it. The employee who thought of the idea was distraught when she informed me about the decision and was near tears. I immediately went to the lawyer to see why. His response was, "Tom, if we allowed this to happen and if a customer at our retail store [located in our building] were to see these segments on our internal TV system, they could interpret it as us violating child labor laws."

My response was something along the lines of, "You cannot be serious?" His retort was, "I'm dead serious." I told the lawyer how unreasonable his decision was and proceeded to tell the events coordinator to air the segments. I began to tell the story to some of my friends, and as I did, I felt embarrassed that I was working at an agency and for an organization that was so backward and obtuse.

If the decision regarding the children's TV segments was probably one of the most blatant internal examples of our lawyer's thinking, then the most blatant external decision involved an online numismatic publication called *Coin News*. The *Coin News* editor, Mike Unser, was an incredible gentleman who was a very successful businessman. One of his passions was coins, and he decided to publish a trade newsletter called *Coin News*.

I admired the publication. It was extremely well-done, professional, and informative. Moreover, it helped the US Mint sell coins and created interest in the numismatic hobby. When I arrived at the Mint in 2009, the nation was trying to recover from a recession. As a result of the depressed economy, coin use was down because people were not spending money. Sales of numismatic products were also down because interest in the numismatic hobby had waned.

Of note, we had just begun to introduce a new quarter that was the follow-on to the hugely successful 50-State Quarter Program. The new coins were to commemorate one national park in each of the 50 states. Since we did not advertise, any help we could get from the media in generating interest in the new coins was most welcome. Also, we were a government agency, and we had an obligation to tell our story—not just about our products but about our 1,800 employees and the work they did.

The new national park quarter introduced in 2010 faced several obstacles and, as a result, was not well received. For instance, everyone could relate in some manner to a state quarter and the imagery on it. Unfortunately, the national park quarter did not carry the same panache and generated a ho-hum type of reaction. Additionally, the economy in 2010 was attempting to recover from the financial crisis that hit in 2008. People were tapping their existing coin supplies (e.g., piggy banks) or simply not making as many cash purchases. Accordingly, the Federal Reserve—the US Mint's customer—was not ordering as many coins. The economic demand for them was not there. In 2010, the first year the national park quarters were released, we only produced 347 million quarters, split evenly between the Philadelphia and Denver mints. As a point of reference, we produced 6.4 billion state quarters in the year 2000. So one can easily see the dramatic difference.

The resultant situation presented a management challenge to US Mint leadership. Was there enough work at both the Philadelphia and Denver facilities to keep everyone fully employed? Were job layoffs going to be necessary? US Mint leadership made the decision to use this opportunity to do maintenance work on the equipment and the facilities, keeping our workers employed while hoping that the economy would turn around and the demand for currency would increase.

Employee morale was poor, and I wanted to help in some way. So I called Mike Unser and essentially gave him a carte blanche invitation to visit all our production facilities—Philadelphia, Denver, San Francisco, and West Point. I had extended the same invitation to other trade publications and national media.

Mike Unser and his brother, Darrin, quickly accepted my offer. Our first visit was to the Philadelphia Mint. The resultant story was extremely positive. The employees he talked to were upbeat and exuded pride in their jobs and the role they played in making products for the US economy. Unser and his brother also took some outstanding photography, both video and still, that captured the entire manufacturing process—from the artists who designed the coins to the coin press operators who operated the vast presses and bagged the coins before shipping them off to the Federal Reserve banks.

Unser was using some costly cameras and lenses he had purchased when he founded *Coin News*. His imagery was nothing like the Mint had ever produced internally. When I told him how impressed I was with his photos and videos, he permitted unrestricted use of his photography—internally or externally. I assured him we would use a photo credit line whenever we used it.

Unser proceeded to visit other US Mint production facilities. Those visits resulted in additional outstanding stories and imagery in *Coin News*. I took a great deal of pride in sending those stories to all our employees as soon as they appeared. In addition to telling the US Mint's story and promoting its products externally, the stories helped immensely in recognizing the outstanding work of Mint employees. Did these stories, along with similar access being provided to other mainstream and numismatic trade media, result in the Mint's rise from 201 (out of about 230 federal agencies being rated at the time as one of the best places to work) to being rated 57th a few years later? I wish I could definitively say.[2]

However, in 2013 the Partnership for Public Service and the Office of Personnel Management (OPM) said we were the most improved federal agency subcomponent and called our turnaround "remarkable."[3] The Partnership cited our communications effort, including use of our own internal TV network—the same one the lawyer did not want us to use.[4]

Conversely, our staff lawyer had a different viewpoint regarding media access and building successful relationships with the press. Unser's understanding and appreciation of the coin making process—and meeting and visiting with many of our employees—was clearly worth the investment of our time. In addition to his outstanding stories, he developed a website (linked though www.CoinNews .net), "America the Beautiful Quarters," and highlighted the national park quarters.[5] The site included a history and background about each park, beautiful photography of the park and imagery Unser had taken at our facilities. Unser's efforts were a way to generate interest in the program, sell numismatic products related to the coin, and educate the public about the history and richness of our national parks. It was a wonderful gift.

Unfortunately, "Dr. No," the staff lawyer, saw it differently. One day in March 2014, he called and said he wanted to meet with me in his office. When I arrived, he displayed a three-page "cease and desist" letter he was planning on sending to Unser, telling him to delete his America the Beautiful Quarters website. The letter contended that the term "America the Beautiful Quarters" was a registered trademark of the US Mint, and we had not authorized Unser's use of the term. The letter was very strident and contained many legal references to US Code, including federal criminal statute violations that could lead to fines or imprisonment. The letter was quite intimidating.

The lawyer told me that he was going to electronically send the letter to Unser in five minutes from our meeting time and wanted to give me a heads-up. I was agitated and told him he should not do this. Unser was a US Mint supporter with whom we had established an excellent rapport. I argued that a more reasonable approach would be to call him on the phone and inform him that his website may be a bit misleading, causing some people to believe Unser's site was a US Mint site.

The lawyer said, "I can't do that, Tom. I have sent similar letters to other violators, and it's important that we be consistent in matters like this."

I said, "But there's a better way to handle this. Why don't we pick up the phone and discuss it with Unser?"

The lawyer was unwilling to compromise. He told me he was going to press "send" in five minutes. I proceeded to run back to my office, leaving fumes in my wake, to call Unser and tell him what was coming. By the time I returned to my office, the damage had been done. I knew Unser had already received the letter when he answered the phone with a sarcastic, "Thanks, Tom."

I was embarrassed. It was a kick in the gut from a teammate. I immediately went to see the US Mint director and informed him how an unreasonable lawyer had potentially destroyed a valuable relationship. Fortunately, the relationship with Unser survived, as a matter of note.

The lawyer and Mint director did meet to discuss the matter. When they met, the director found out that this was not the first time the lawyer had sent similar "cease and desist" letters to coin dealers and other entities.

This entire matter could have been handled differently. It is almost as if the lawyer wanted the Mint to fail—to continue its poor morale and weak understanding of its role in the American landscape. I readily admit that this matter is an extreme example, but it illustrates what happens when a key staff member goes rogue and decides not to be a team player by keeping leadership uninformed of potential adverse actions. Quite simply, it is not the way to do business. It is not only unprofessional but also what I consider disloyal. Lawyers are staff members and supposed to work together as a team with other members of that staff, coordinating and communicating as they perform their duties.

It is interesting to note that the lawyer, in addition to our weekly staff meeting, had a weekly one-on-one meeting with the Mint director. The lawyer had every opportunity to inform the director and the staff of his strident and intimidating cease and desist letters. However, he chose not to and elected to blindside his own team members.

Was this a leadership failure? An awareness failure within the organization? Perhaps. It was clear the lawyer—dissimilar from many of those I had worked with elsewhere throughout my career—did not understand the role of the media and the added value good media relationships could bring to the Mint. We had worked hard to develop and nurture a friendship with the media, but the lawyer saw it differently and felt it was better to write legalese letters that could intimidate.

The Takeaway

Leadership needs to be aware of staff actions, needs to be engaged, and must require that staff members share information on actions constantly. Conversely, staff members need to be team players, and those who do not "play well with others" and damage the organization need to be rooted out.

Staff members also need to have an understanding of the role and responsibilities of fellow staff members. This, too, is a function of leadership, and leadership must facilitate this type of interaction and ensure it occurs. The health and well-being of any organization depend on it.

Notes

1. Partnership for Public Service, "Ten Years of the Best Places to Work in the Federal Government Rankings," 16–18.
2. Partnership for Public Service, "Ten Years of the Best Places to Work in the Federal Government Rankings," 16–18.
3. Partnership for Public Service, "Ten Years of the Best Places to Work in the Federal Government Rankings," 16–18.
4. Partnership for Public Service, "Ten Years of the Best Places to Work in the Federal Government Rankings," 16–18.
5. "America the Beautiful Quarters." See the "Hot Springs National Park Quarter."

Chapter 11

Leadership
What It Is and What It Isn't

During my professional career, I have been blessed working with and for several great leaders. I have learned many things from them. I have also observed several people who made me shake my head and say to myself, "If ever given a chance to lead, I will not be like that guy." Nevertheless, I learned from the weak leaders as well—for example, what not to emulate and how not to treat people.

I have had a penchant for documenting some of the classic tenets of what I think represents good leadership fundamentals. Whenever I see something that I think documents sound leadership principles, I throw it in a folder.

One of the most exceptional pieces that defines leadership is found in the book *African Laughter* by Doris Lessing.[1] Lessing was a white British novelist, poet, playwright, and short-story writer. She won a Nobel Prize for literature in 2007. After that short description of her, a common reaction might be, "What does Doris Lessing know about leadership?"

Lessing was born in Iran, moved to Southern Rhodesia when she was about six years old, and lived there for about 25 years before moving to London. During her time in Southern Rhodesia (now Zimbabwe), Lessing developed some fond memories and returned to Zimbabwe four times. In *African Laughter,* she recounts those four visits after being exiled from Southern Rhodesia for her opposition to the white minority government.

In her last visit, in 1992, Lessing presented a pessimistic view of the Robert Mugabe regime that had taken over the country's government. During that visit, she noticed tensions that existed between the whites and the blacks. The whites that remained in Zimbabwe after its independence were critical of the blacks and longed for the days when whites ruled. She noticed intense hostility.

For example, on one occasion, when Lessing encountered a pregnant black woman on the street, her white friends warned her not to give the woman a ride. She did give her a ride and at the time heard her brother refer to blacks as "inferior."

Upon visiting a Zimbabwe government office, Lessing noticed a poster on the wall that contrasted a black *leader* and a white *boss*. The poster read:

The Boss drives his men,

The Leader inspires them.

The Boss depends on authority.

The Leader depends on goodwill.

The Boss evokes fear,

The Leader radiates love.

The Boss says, "I."

The Leader says, "We."

The Boss shows who is wrong.

The Leader shows what is wrong.

The Boss knows how it is done.

The Leader knows how to do it.

The Boss demands respect.

The Leader commands respect.

So be a leader,

Not a boss.[2]

The health, happiness, and productivity of many organizations in today's world can be measured by the words on the poster Lessing saw at the government office in Zimbabwe. So-called leaders that lead by fear and intimidation do not have any knowledge about the people who work for them—their marriage status, where they live, or how many children they have. They refuse to leave their office and mingle with the troops.

I once worked for an individual who practiced "coaching" as part of our professional and personal development. In one of our sessions, he asked me what he could do to be a better leader. I told him that he needed to get away from his computer and mingle with the troops—say "hi" and ask people about their current projects. I told him, "Be visible and show our folks that you're interested in them and what they're doing. Tell them you appreciate what they do every day to make our organization successful." Some people associate such a leadership tool with what I term *management by walking around*. "I can't do that, Tom," he said. "I feel I would be interjecting myself in the chain of command."

I could not believe what I had just heard. I was in disbelief. I knew right then why this leader had a poor reputation and commanded little respect. He was looked upon as arrogant and uncaring.

One of the leaders I most enjoyed working for was Admiral Larson. I worked for him at both the US Pacific Fleet headquarters in Pearl Harbor, Hawaii, and then again at the US Naval Academy in Annapolis, Maryland.

When Larson retired as commander of the Pacific Command, any number of Fortune 500 companies would have warmly welcomed him as a member of its executive team or board of directors. He had established himself as not only an outstanding naval officer but also a diplomat. He commanded respect, and he knew how to lead.

Instead of joining the private sector, Larson chose to return to the Naval Academy and continue his commitment to public service by restoring the school's image. He wanted to ensure it remained rooted in integrity, character, and honor. Larson knew even before he arrived back in Annapolis in August 1994 that he had some "fixing" to do. We have documented the successful repair of some of those issues earlier in the book.

One of the fixes was ensuring the school developed leaders. Larson felt the Naval Academy had drifted from this significant core value and objective. When he returned, Larson sensed a cultural change on the part of midshipmen had fallen upon the Academy. An air of arrogance was prevalent. For the school to return to its roots, this arrogance had to be eliminated. He knew the key to success in returning to those roots depended upon the midshipmen. Larson felt the school needed to ensure its graduates, future Navy and Marine Corps officers, understood they were the same as officers from other commissioning sources (e.g., Navy ROTC and OCS)—just better prepared as leaders.

Larson interestingly referred to the Academy as a leadership laboratory—a place where future officers could develop their leadership techniques. The midshipmen students had to learn how to follow before they learned how to lead. Larson always told the midshipmen that they had four years to develop their initial set of leadership tools and techniques, learning from those whom they viewed as effective leaders and those they saw as ineffective leaders.

In short, Larson felt that the Academy needed to develop future officers who were committed to excellence—but committed to excellence without arrogance. To do so, Larson put together 10 guiding principles that demanded buy-in. We put those principles on posters and provided them to each midshipman and staff member. Although developed for the Naval Academy, the principles have clear relevance to anyone who aspires to be a leader and outline how we all should live our lives. Those principles are as follows:

> *Uphold the standards of the Naval Academy [insert name of any organization].*
>
> *Be a person of integrity.*
>
> *Lead by example (meet the standard you are holding others to).*
>
> *Strive for excellence without arrogance.*
>
> *Do your best.*
>
> *Treat everyone with dignity and respect.*
>
> *Tolerate honest mistakes from people who are doing their best.*
>
> *Speak well of others (gossip undermines human dignity).*
>
> *Seek the truth (rumors and unverified anecdotes undermine morale).*
>
> *Keep a sense of humor and be able to laugh at yourself.*

When I changed careers—moved into the private sector and then returned to the government as a civilian employee—I ensured that the poster of Larson's principles was with me and hung it in my office in a prominent location. When I met with subordinates or peers, I frequently pointed to the poster and reminded them of a pertinent principle. They are genuinely principles all leaders—and anyone who aspires to be a leader—should practice daily.

Larson's leadership style favored humility. The *Wall Street Journal*, citing several studies, contends "humility is a core quality of leaders who inspire close teamwork, rapid learning, and high performance in their teams."[3]

The head of human resources for a global hotel chain says that humility is an emotional skill leaders need to have. Humility gives rise to deep listening, respect for diverse views, and a willingness to hear suggestions and feedback. A human resources researcher added that teams with humble leaders performed better and did higher-quality work than teams whose leaders exhibited less humility.[4]

There are other nuggets on leadership that I have filed away that are also essential tenets by which leaders *must* abide.

- *Empower the people that work for you.* Doing so gives your employees confidence in themselves. Let them know that when you are empowering them to do a job, you are doing so because you have faith in them to do that job, and you will not let them fail. I remember hearing a government executive once say that leaders should let employees "fall over the cliff and fail with an assignment." She contended that it would be a great learning experience.

  NO. NO. NO. That is not the right approach to leadership. Making mistakes is okay and should be tolerated, but a good leader monitors a subordinate and allows him or her to do a task and will never allow that employee to fall off the cliff.

- *Trust your employees.* Trusting them will give them confidence, and it will also generate loyalty. I have always found loyalty to be a critical component of an organization's health. I once considered hiring someone to be my deputy. One of my subordinates said that person X was smarter than the individual I wanted to hire, but I questioned person X's loyalty to the organization and me when or if the going got a little rough. My subordinate said that to him, smarts were better than loyalty. Sorry. I will forever disagree. Loyal employees will always tell you what you need to hear as a leader—not what you may want to hear. I am never confident in the motives of a person who may not be loyal to you, your organization, or both. Quite simply, I am not prone to hiring self-serving individuals.

  Another technique to show trust may be to allow your employees to do a briefing at a staff meeting that you, as the leader, usually attend. For example, let him or her brief a project on which they have been working. The information will be well received by your peers and will reflect on you as the leader of your team. Your peers will see you as providing an opportunity to show off your team and your belief in your staff. It also sends a positive signal to your employees about the trust you have in them.

If you assign a project, assign it to one subordinate—not two or three others, too. I have observed several of my colleagues and other leaders who assign the same project to two or three employees. Unbeknownst to the employee, the supervisor/leader is trying to see who comes back with a completed effort the soonest. When the subordinates learn what the leader has done, they become deflated and angry—and rightly so. The leader/supervisor has just caused a morale issue and dug himself or herself into a hole that he or she may not even realize. These are the same type of leaders who thrive on creating an atmosphere of fear. Unfortunately, this type of environment stymies creativity and collaboration—some of which could benefit the organization.

Look out for your employees and get to know them. Be interested in them. Know their marriage status. Know how many kids they have. Know where they went to school. Become familiar with their hobbies and interests and know when their birthdays are so you can acknowledge them on that day.

- When I was a junior officer on my first ship and had 40 sailors in my division, I did not know how to repair a winch or repair the four boats we had onboard that would take sailors ashore when we made port visits. I knew my senior enlisted staff would ensure repairs or maintenance was accomplished correctly, but I made sure their berthing compartment was clean. I also made sure I knew when they were scheduled to take their next advancement exam—and that they were studying for it. I also made sure I knew their names, where they were from, and something about their families. Those little gestures told them I cared about them. I found that they grew comfortable with me and would come to me with personal problems or issues.

- Similarly, I knew the manager of a well-known national retail store. The company had an excellent reputation with both its customers and employees. The company offered its employees excellent benefits, but an individual had to work with the chain for one year before they became eligible for disability pay. One of the employees—a single parent who was three weeks shy of being with the company for one year—suffered domestic violence by her boyfriend. Her injuries were severe, including a concussion and severe facial injuries. She was not able to work for several weeks. The store manager wrote an email to corporate headquarters and stated what a great employee this individual was—one of the store's top salespersons and a committed and loyal employee who had not missed a day of work since she first signed on. The manager strongly articulated the employee's worth, not just to the store, but also to the company and requested that she be considered for disability pay. The company waived its policy and awarded 75 percent of her weekly salary. The employee was thrilled and grateful that her store manager made an effort to obtain a waiver. Her already healthy level of loyalty to the company was most likely strengthened immeasurably.

Be honest and direct with your employees. One of the things subordinates want is feedback. What are the qualities that make them strong performing employees? What are their weaknesses? What can they improve upon to be better members of the team? Too often, supervisors/leaders are afraid to provide criticism of their subordinates. Even during annual performance review sessions, leaders/supervisors regurgitate all the positive things they have written. Leaders often shy away from offering even constructive criticism. The time to offer that criticism, however, is not during annual review periods. A good leader will offer guidance, direction, and help throughout the year—not just at mid-year review or final appraisal time. You will be surprised how much constructive criticism or guidance is welcomed continuously. Constructive criticism can always be mixed with kudos to soften the possible impact.

Do not tolerate poor performers. One of the worst things a leader can do is continue to employ poor performers. Most high performing employees do not want them on the team. Take action with poor performers. If it means their behavior must be documented to take action, do it! Poor performers are a drain on the team and result in lousy morale—a cancer—that affects good performers. Not taking action on poor performers will ultimately reflect on you—the leader. The effectiveness of the team—its product, performance, and creativity—will suffer. Taking action will send a positive signal to your good performers that you care about them.

Do not forget to pause and say the little things. Small words of praise or expressions of interest go a long way. Examples:

"Great job."

"Thank you for sharing your idea at our last staff meeting. I'm going to consider it."

"What are you working on today?"

"How was your vacation with the family?"

"How's that evening course you're taking?"

"When is graduation?"

"Are you enjoying it?"

"How's the baby? And is your wife doing okay?"

Be Passionate. Being passionate and energetic about your job is contagious. When your employees see passion and energy in their leader, they will want to duplicate it. If employees see you as not "buying-in" to a specific project or program, then they are not going to buy-in either. Why should they?

Maintain your integrity and honesty. Be honest with your employees, and be everything you want them to be. If your organization has a set of core values, abide by those values and show commitment to them. If employees know you have a family and witness that you are having an affair, then you have dug yourself into a hole—at least with some employees. You may have lost the respect of many employees.

A trusted colleague related to me that he found himself in a situation where his immediate boss was having an extramarital affair. It occurred to him that not only did he now have a lack of respect regarding his boss but also he felt he could not trust him. He said, "If he is going to lie and cheat on his wife, then what's to keep him from treating me the same?" He said he always kept an eye on his boss to avoid being collateral damage because of the boss's untrustworthy behavior.

Also, if you say you are going to do something, do not just offer lip service to your team. Do it, or at least try to get it done. Follow through on your commitments. It may be something as small as following through on complaints about office cleanliness or a dirty microwave in the lunchroom.

Be an effective communicator. Hopefully, your employees understand the goals and vision of the organization. Nevertheless, what are your goals and vision for your team? Share them and share how you feel your team can meet them. When you attend your weekly staff meetings with other department or division leaders, provide your team feedback from those meetings. I always tried to schedule my department or staff meetings on the same day I had the larger organizational meetings with the head of the organization or agency. This allowed my employees to feel plugged-in to what was going on. By sharing information, you are also saying you respect your employees and you value them as a member of the overall team.

Be an ardent listener. Some individuals contend that being a good listener equates to being a good leader. Letting people share their ideas and respectfully receiving them is crucial and sends a powerful signal to your team. It says you respect your employees, and you value their ideas. Also, there is usually more than one way to do a job, and often the idea to do it another way comes from your employees—if you listen objectively. However, you need to not only listen but also act on those ideas. If an idea does not work, you need to say why. On the other hand, if an idea has merit, you need to follow through and not let it linger unaddressed. Keep your team apprised of its status.

Be decisive. Being a leader means having to make decisions—but subordinates do not necessarily welcome all decisions. Leaders have to accept the fact they are not going to be able to please everyone. The worst thing a leader can do is be wishy-washy and unable or unwilling to make a decision. Often, leaders will try to build consensus, perhaps buying time in the hope a problem or issue will go away. That does not work, builds resentment, and causes a leader to lose the respect of his or her team.

In 2016 the spokesman for CNO Adm John Richardson was at a Christmas party in the Pentagon dressed as Santa Claus. Apparently, under the influence of alcohol, the Navy commander allegedly slapped a civilian woman's buttocks and then made sexual advances in a "predatory" way toward subordinate officers.[5] It took Richardson eight months to remove the offending officer from his staff and move him to a nonsupervisory position.

Because of Richardson's failure to act quickly and more aggressively to the situation, *USA Today* became aware of the situation and reported on the alleged behavior and lack of action. The matter caught the attention of the DOD Office of the Inspector General (OIG), who initiated an investigation into the slowness of the removal of the officer from the CNO's staff. What resulted was another *USA Today* story when the DOD OIG released its report that rebuked Richardson for mishandling the matter.[6]

The obvious question is, "What was the CNO thinking by keeping the officer on his staff?" With all the issues arising from the #MeToo movement, most people would think this would have been an easy decision for him. Additionally, all the military services have been under a tremendous amount of scrutiny because of sexual assaults and improper behavior towards women. Not taking action and letting specific incidents linger adds more fuel to the fires. If nothing else, it provides evidence to congressional leaders that the military services turn a blind eye to and tolerate inappropriate behavior.

Interestingly, Richardson told the DOD investigators he was following the advice of his lawyers in keeping the officer on his staff.[7] I would argue that legal advice sometimes does not pass the sniff test. In other words, legal advice is just that; you do not have to take it.

And Sometimes Leadership Just Means *THINK* Before You Speak

In today's parlance, there is a phrase that some people use to characterize many things, and the phrase is, "They just don't get it. What in the hell were they thinking?" Those words frequently capture the actions of a company, a politician, a public servant—or even a four-star admiral.

For example, I will never forget when I was on the Pacific Fleet staff, Adm Robert J. Kelly, the fleet commander, had just returned from a meeting of four-star admirals in Washington. These meetings occurred regularly, and Kelly would always debrief the staff about what was discussed at these meetings. The feedback was precious and most welcomed. This particular meeting was significant, though, because it occurred after Tailhook '91. The Navy was still recovering from the aftermath, and there seemed to be a heightened sensitivity about everything.

Just before providing his debrief, Kelly said he had a joke to share that he heard at the four-star meeting. It went like this;

> A guy was driving home after a party celebrating his 55th birthday. He had a flat, and while changing the tire, a frog jumped up on his lap and said, "Hi. I'm a talking frog." And the guy says, "My goodness, I've never seen a talking frog. What do you do?" The frog says, "I'm a genie. I'll tell you what. If you let me go, I'll make your manhood grow by two inches." So the guy puts the frog in his pocket, and the frog jumps out and says, "Hey, let me go." And the guy looks in his pocket and says, "At my age, I'd rather have a talking frog."

There was stunned silence in the room. I looked at senior officers to my immediate left and right, and there were female staff members in both seats. There were other females in the room as well, and all I remember thinking to myself was, "What in the hell is this guy thinking? Why not just keep this joke to himself?"

I think when Kelly heard mostly silence and perhaps just a few under the breath chuckles, he realized the error of his ways. He then said, "Well, I guess we'll be reading about that one in tomorrow's *San Diego Union.*"

It was not the next day—but pretty close to it. I was sitting in my office at about 11 a.m., and I was about ready to leave my office to go home and pick up my family. We had made plans to visit the Big Island (Hawaii), and my wife and two girls were very excited. The office phone rang, and my administrative assistant said it was reporter Greg Vistica. I knew Greg very well, of course. So I took the call and it went something like this:

"So Tom, tell me about the talking frog. I hear he has some magical powers."

I was not surprised. Kelly was not the most well-liked fleet commander. Many people resented him for multiple reasons—primarily his harsh treatment of fellow staff members. I was also angry because I saw my family trip and my precious family time "going down the drain." Nevertheless, we "fessed up," admitted to the joke (about 40 people heard it), and apologized. However, the damage had been done—not to mention its becoming another story in the *San Diego Union* about Navy leadership being insensitive and its prevalent macho culture.

Despite the situation, my family and I were able to go on our visit to the Big Island, but I was on edge the entire weekend and had to handle a seemingly endless number of phone calls. The story ran while I was away, and there was not much I could do at that point except confirm the details and respond to other media interests with the same apology.

Another "what were they thinking?" four-star moment occurred in 1995—with Tailhook '91 still quite visible in the Navy's rear view mirror. Adm Richard Macke, the four-star commander of the entire Pacific region, had just attended a meeting with the media in Washington.

One of the issues discussed at the wide-ranging session was the arrest of three Marines for raping a 12-year-old girl on Okinawa. One of the last remarks he was quoted as saying—almost in passing because some of the media had already departed—was "It was absolutely stupid," referring to the rape. "I've said several times, for the price they [the service members] paid to rent the car, they could have had a girl."

In essence, Macke said the Marines could have avoided the rape by merely paying for a prostitute, but it struck many of the reporters as another example of a senior Navy leader being insensitive to sexual misconduct and international relations with the host nation of Japan.

A female reporter from the Hearst newspaper chain heard the remark and reported it almost immediately. It did not take much longer (mere hours) for Macke to retire. Macke should have been much more sensitive at this point in his career—especially after Tailhook '91 and the sensitivity training the Navy instituted.

Both Kelly and Macke fell under the "what were they thinking?" category—especially as four-star admirals. They should have thought about what they were going to say before they opened their mouths. You do not have to be a four-star admiral to realize that fact. Anyone in a leadership position needs to have heightened sensitivity to their words and actions. It harkens back to one of the things most parents taught us when we were younger: *Think before you speak.*

The Takeaway

Leadership encompasses numerous forms and entails a myriad of elements. In essence, it all comes down to *people.* How you manage them, how you care for them, how you treat them, how you communicate and talk to them, and how you inspire them will help you and your organization possess passion and make an impact.

Trust your employees. *Let them run,* allow them to make mistakes and learn from those mistakes. Demonstrate that trust by giving them responsibility. Empower your employees. Then watch and monitor your employees as they complete the tasks you have assigned. Coach along the way and be supportive by reminding them you want them to succeed.

Notes

1. Lessing, *African Laughter.*
2. Lessing, *African Laughter,* 231.
3. Shellenberger, "The Best Bosses Are Humble Bosses," A11.
4. Shellenberger, A11.
5. Vanden Brook, "Bad Santa."
6. Vanden Brook.
7. Vanden Brook.

Chapter 12

Crisis Communications

The True Test of an Organization

Just for curiosity's sake, use an internet search engine and insert the term *crisis communications* and see what populates. What you will find is an enormous list of entries. It is interesting that the first several entries most likely to appear are advertisements by firms that offer crisis communications services to companies, organizations, or individuals who find themselves facing reputation-damaging situations.

When I was the PA officer at the US Naval Academy and was faced with the string of untoward incidents discussed in earlier chapters—a drug ring, a car theft ring, a midshipman accused of pedophilia, midshipmen who broke into a home that happened to be the residence of the Maryland State Police superintendent, and a murder, to name a few—I was besieged by calls from numerous PR agencies who wanted to "turn our image around." I was professionally offended, but I politely declined the offers. I also knew that if we hired a PR firm, that in itself would be another story—a story that would make the American taxpayer irate.

What I did—with the consent of Admiral Larson—was to put together a panel of PR professionals from the Washington, DC, and Baltimore areas. I knew that between the various trade organizations and corporations in the region, we could put together a distinguished group of savvy individuals. My objectives for them were to visit the Academy, spend some time with us, and see our internal and external communications efforts. I wanted them to speak to faculty members and midshipmen and assess what we may be doing right as well as what we may be doing wrong. Then we would offer an assessment of our efforts.

I invited senior executives from a variety of companies. This included such companies as McCormick Spices, The Business Roundtable, Mobil Oil (it had not yet merged with Exxon), General Dynamics, Giant Food, and Crown Central Petroleum. When I spoke with the executives, I mentioned our challenges encountered at the Academy—they were all familiar with them—and explained that we were putting together an advisory panel. We asked if they would participate on a gratis basis. Virtually all the participants were eager to offer their counsel.

At our first meeting, Admiral Larson spoke to the group and outlined his vision and goal of restoring ethics and leadership at the Academy. I provided an overview of our communications efforts and how we were responding to the variety of crises we were facing—including the adverse incidents that had occurred before Larson's leadership of the school—the chaining of a woman to male urinals and a cheating scandal involving more than 100 students.

In a nutshell, the group of experts we put together gave us a clean bill of health. What they zeroed in on was *how* we responded to various situations and asked:

- Did we respond quickly, or did we try to pretend nothing happened and put our head in the sand? Did we think the problem would just go away?

- Were we forthcoming and transparent?

- Did we provide media access to students and faculty?

- Did we keep faculty and staff informed of the crises and our proposed plan of action?

Receiving the group's validation for our method of pursuing action was reassuring, but it also enabled us to establish a relationship with these executives who were volunteering their expertise and time. The experts, without exception, told us to contact them anytime for advice or a "sanity check." This included ideas or initiatives encountered as we pursued Admiral Larson's goals and any new crisis that might arise.

Crisis Responses

There have been books, monographs, presentations, papers, and countless case studies that document both excellent and inadequate responses to crises. We will start with by focusing on a list of notable successes and then move into a series of notable failures.

Notable Successes

The Tylenol Tampering Case[1]

This stands as the benchmark example of how to respond to a crisis. In 1982, seven people died after taking Extra Strength Tylenol tablets from bottles that contained cyanide. Johnson & Johnson immediately pulled more than 30 million bottles of the medication off its shelves. Johnson & Johnson designed and introduced a new tamper-proof bottle along with a significant PR and advertising efforts to regain customers. The makers of Tylenol announced a $100,000 reward; however, Johnson & Johnson never found a perpetrator. Nevertheless, the brand recovered beautifully—primarily because Johnson & Johnson acknowledged the issue, took quick action, was seen as a victim, developed tamper-proof packaging, and communicated often and well with the public via the news media.

Pepsi Responded to a False Allegation in 1993[2]

To respond to an allegation that a consumer found a syringe in a can of Pepsi in 1993, Pepsi worked with the Food and Drug Administration (FDA) and produced four videos that showed the canning safety process at its production facilities. The videos also depicted how quickly the cans go through the process—being closed in a blink of an eye after they are filled. It is not possible for a syringe to be placed in a can in that short period. Pepsi's CEO and the head of the FDA appeared on ABC's *Nightline* to debunk the allegations. Ironically, a store camera caught a customer trying to stick a needle into a Pepsi can. That put an end to the crisis.

The 2003 Discovery of Worms in Cadbury Chocolate Bars[3]

After consumers discovered worms in two Cadbury chocolate bars in India, the Indian government's equivalent of the FDA seized the chocolate stock at a Cadbury manufacturing plant. Cadbury initially said the worms could not have been incorporated into the candy. The Indian FDA disagreed. The media covered the story extensively, and Cadbury found itself under a lot of unwanted media attention and pressure. Cadbury removed its on-air advertising and instead initiated an educational PR program for its retailers—about 200,000 of them. Cadbury kept the media informed and updated on precisely what it was doing to correct the manufacturing and the storage of chocolate. Cadbury ordered and installed new machinery and changed the packaging process of chocolate bars. They initiated a new advertising program featuring the candy and Cadbury slowly began to rebound in India, ultimately regaining its top position in the Indian chocolate market.

Conversely, there have been countless situations that were handled inadequately.

Notable Failures

Domino's Pizza Employees Picked Their Noses[4]

In 2009, two Dominoes employees uploaded a video where they picked their noses, sneezed on pizzas, and completed other bodily functions as they prepared pizzas. The two employees were fired after two days and ultimately, criminally charged. This was one of the first cases that demonstrated the power of the internet and social media. News media across the country shared the story, more than one million people viewed the video on YouTube, and criticism of Domino's consumed Twitter. The company waited two days to take action and such a delay severely damaged the company's reputation. The video remains on YouTube. The company should have acted immediately; however, they waited far too long to respond to the situation.

Wells Fargo Employees Created Two Million Fake Accounts[5]

To meet sales goals in 2016, Wells Fargo employees created two million fake accounts. The revelation about the employees' actions created a media firestorm. The CEO of the bank, John Stumpf, was required to testify before the Senate Banking Committee several weeks after the disclosure. However, it was not until his congressional testimony that he said he was "deeply sorry"—and then only after being grilled by senators. Additionally, he did not take responsibility as the leader and blamed the 5,100 employees who were involved and subsequently fired. Stumpf never addressed Wells Fargo's corporate policy on fraud, the lack of oversight, or accountability by corporate leadership that would allow such behavior to go on unchecked.

Allegations That One of Tesco's Suppliers Was Replacing Beef with Horsemeat[6]

Tesco is a sizable British chain of grocery stores. In 2013, soon after the allegations went public, Tesco tweeted the following: "It's sleepy time so we're off to the hay! See you at 8 a.m. for more #TescoTweets."[7] Tesco apologized, said the tweet had been previously scheduled and noted that the copy was written days before the allegations. Unfortunately, someone in the communications department was not paying attention to detail by allowing such insensitive communication to be transmitted. *Hay* is not a word you want to hear or read in a tweet when your company is being charged with selling horsemeat as beef.

The *Good, the Bad, and The Ugly* . . . Examining Leadership in the Airline Business

The Good

JetBlue's Handling of Problems Following a Significant East Coast Ice Storm in 2007[8]

The airline had to cancel approximately 1,000 flights over five days as a result of the storm. During the early hours of this crisis in New York, the airline chose to keep passengers seated on planes on runways for up to 11 hours instead of busing them back to the terminal. The CEO, David G. Neeleman, said the company was at fault instead of blaming the weather and apologized to customers. The airline then wrote letters of apology to customers and introduced a customer's bill of rights, which included monetary compensation. Neeleman took his case public and went on YouTube, the *Today Show, Letterman,* and CNN to apologize for how inadequately Jet-Blue responded to the storm.

How to Do It Right—Southwest Airlines—Above and Beyond

When it comes to airlines, Southwest is one that I think has its act together, both from PR and customer relations standpoints. In fact, in many cases, the two are closely intertwined. I have flown on Southwest often. Whenever I have been inconvenienced because of weather or a mechanical issue, I have found a gift voucher in my email within a day or two, apologizing for the delay. I am not sure what the parameters are for issuing the vouchers, but none of the other airlines I have flown has ever done that.

I have also found Southwest flight crews, both in the cockpit and cabin, to be friendly and courteous—sometimes downright funny. They certainly have a way of making nervous flyers much more comfortable and happy—both on the ground and in the air. It is *those* actions, the humor and the smiles that reflect good leadership and training—unlike a United incident documented later in this chapter.

Southwest Airlines' Appropriate Response to a Tragic Inflight Incident

On 17 April 2018, a Southwest flight from New York to Dallas suffered a catastrophic engine failure. Shrapnel from the engine broke through a window on the aircraft, causing a passenger to be partially sucked out of the window. The plane proceeded to land safely in Philadelphia; however, the passenger died. Although the events that occurred were tragic, what happened next was most impressive in terms of leadership. All Southwest executives were attending a leadership development conference in Dallas when they were notified of the incident. The conference was immediately suspended, and the executives moved to its nearby headquarters where they put an emergency response plan into action.

The *Wall Street Journal* said it best: "How companies respond to crises, especially those broadcast live and spread worldwide on social media, has become a major test." Instantaneous posting to social media of cell phone videos have made airline incidents and any catastrophe or incident even more problematic for a company or organization.

The *Wall Street Journal* documented Southwest's response to the tragedy by highlighting actions employed by the airline:[9]

- The CEO immediately delivered a 40-second apology and showed contrition through honest and heartfelt condolences.

- The airline issued multiple updates with new facts.

- Behind the scenes, Southwest made sure it had resources in Philadelphia where the plane landed to take care of passengers.

- The airline immediately sent a plane from Dallas to Philadelphia with employees who were part of an accident response "go team."

- Some of those employees were assigned to help customers with travel arrangements. Other employees were available to provide trauma counseling.

- Southwest sent four employees to Albuquerque to provide support to the family of the deceased passenger.

- Southwest made arrangements for those passengers who chose to remain in Philadelphia overnight. It also placed letters under their hotel doors to remind them that assistance and counseling were available.

- On the second day, all passengers on the original flight received calls and emails to once again remind them of available assistance and counseling that Southwest was offering.

- Each passenger on the original flight then received a $5,000 check plus a $1,000 Southwest flight voucher.

Southwest's response to the accident was "textbook" and should serve as a model for any organization. The airline had a crisis communications plan and updated it regularly, in addition to regularly conducting exercises to practice the plan.

"There's no formula except compassion. This is something that we know we will always do, and so we want to be quick," said Southwest's senior manager of emergency response.[10] A former airline communications executive added, "Nothing kills a negative story faster than doing the right thing and making people feel treated with respect."[11]

The Bad

United Airlines Forcibly Removed a Passenger from an Overbooked Flight in 2017[12]

The incident occurred when United overbooked a flight, and the flight crew asked for four volunteers to give up their seats so that several United employees could make other connections. When an insufficient number of passengers volunteered, the crew said they were going to have to pick four passengers at random. One of the passengers picked happened to be a medical doctor. He said he had patients waiting for him and was not going to give up his seat. A uniformed security officer then forcibly removed him from the plane, physically harming him in the process. Another passenger documented the incident via video and it went viral on social media. United Airlines' then CEO, Oscar Munoz, made the incident worse by apologizing for "reaccommodating" the passengers.[13] To some people, "reaccommodating" translated to dragging people off an aircraft. Munoz also said United was going to contact the doctor to address and resolve the situation; however, there was nothing to resolve. The apology seemed empty, especially to those who were on the plane. They saw what happened, as did millions who saw the video on social media. Neither Munoz nor the United staff handled the situation properly. They did not reveal its culpability for its improper actions. The actions of the crew reflected shoddy judgment, substandard leadership, and a lack of training. The end result was a loss of $800 million in United revenue. The clear lesson here is that when apologizing for the actions of your company, firm, or entity, do so with substance and emotion. "Say it like you mean it," as the saying goes. Follow up the apology by stating that such an incident will never happen again. If you take corrective actions, say so. Furthermore, if you discipline or fire employees, say that too. Standing up and being accountable goes a lot further than coming up with a bunch of hollow words.

The Ugly

How *Not* to Do it—Boeing and the 737 Max

In stark contrast to how Southwest handled its accident is how Boeing handled the crashes of two 737 Max aircraft. Nearly 350 passengers and crew died when a Lion Air 737 Max and an Ethiopian Airlines 737 Max crashed within five months of one another—in October 2018 and March 2019 respectively.[14]

After the second crash, authorities grounded the 737 Max worldwide, leading to one of commercial aviation's largest crises.[15] What ensued, however, was a total dismantlement of Boeing's sterling reputation as a global company that prided itself on safety and innovation. The company made several mistakes that led to its suffering blows both financially and to its brand reputation.

First and foremost, it took a week after the second accident for Boeing's CEO at the time, Dennis Muilenburg, to issue a statement on the investigation of the Ethiopian Airlines crash. To wait a week to express a company's sympathies to the families and loved ones of those who died is simply unacceptable. This long wait could very well have been at the recommendation of lawyers who were fearful of how such a statement could be used against the company. If true—this was totally the wrong reaction. As we've discussed, sometimes the advice of lawyers is just that—advice. It does not have to be taken. Common sense, human courtesy, and compassion will almost always trump the advice of lawyers.

The Boeing statement went on to note its support of the investigation into the crash. The statement indicated "safety is our highest priority as we design, build and support our airplane."[16] Unfortunately, as the investigations into the two accidents continued, it became obvious that safety was *not* the highest priority of how the 737 Max was designed and built. What became apparent as the weeks and months unfolded was that Boeing ignored safety concerns and subordinated those concerns to profitability when building the airplane.

Boeing developed and installed a flawed flight control system (called MCAS) that forced both the Lion Air and Ethiopian Airlines planes into uncontrollable nose dives. When additional testing revealed this discrepancy, pilots who had flown Boeing planes for years—both in the military and commercially—became outraged because Boeing never told the pilots the faulty system even existed.[17]

The outrage only grew when Boeing initially defended the design and suggested pilot errors were to blame for the crashes. Revelations that Boeing officials knew about the system flaws before the crashes and appeared to have paid little attention to those concerns only exacerbated the situation.

An American Airlines test pilot said he had been flying Boeing products for 33 years. He said at one time there was a saying that "If it ain't Boeing, I ain't going." But he said that high level of confidence has been lost. "They horridly fouled up this aircraft."[18]

Airline customers expressed similar sentiments. A survey of about 2,000 air travelers showed that more than 80 percent said they would avoid flying on a 737 Max within its first six months back on the flight deck. More than half of the respondents said they would pay a higher fare just to avoid flying on a Max.[19]

Boeing worsened the entire issue when it released a raft of internal documents in a congressional hearing that painted an even fuller picture of design errors that contributed to the two crashes. The documents reaffirmed management's disregard for safety warnings from subordinates that began years before the crashes.[20]

At the request of Congress, Boeing subsequently released hundreds more internal messages that further damaged the company. Some of the internal communications dated back to 2013. They revealed that employees had concerns about management's strong resistance to mandatory simulator training for Max pilots and the plane's new flight control system.[21] Boeing executives were concerned that the new flight control system might trigger additional training requirements if regulators focused on its details: "If you emphasize MCAS is a new function, there may be a greater certification and training impact," said notes from a meeting.[22] Putting pilots through simulator sessions is expensive and time-consuming. In its competition with Airbus, Boeing made it a selling point of the Max that it would not require upfront simulator training.[23] Boeing's chief test pilot, in fact, aggressively sought to convince some regulators and customers that extra simulator sessions for the Max were not necessary: "I want to stress the importance of holding firm that there will not be any type of simulator training required. Boeing will not allow that to happen. We'll go toe to toe with any regulator who tried to make that a requirement."[24] An employee, in an exchange that illustrated a difference in opinion about the need for simulator training, said, "Our arrogance is our demise."[25] Another said, "I still haven't been forgiven by God for the covering up I did last year" for manipulating regulators.[26]

The bottom line is that the Boeing leadership culture prioritized costs over safety, emphasized cost cutting, and strived only to meet shareholder value. Some employees saw that Boeing's disregard for poor design led to safety concerns and management had the opportunity to step in and address those concerns. However, Boeing basically cast employee input and concerns to the curb: "This airplane is designed by clowns who in turn are supervised by monkeys," one employee wrote in 2017.[27]

The released documents demonstrate a disturbing picture of how far Boeing was apparently willing to go to in order to avoid scrutiny from regulators, flight crews, and the flying public—even as its own employees were sounding alarms internally. Boeing did not want its customers to die—it just had a misplaced sense of values that prioritized profit over safety and minimized the risks involved.

Somewhat shocking was Boeing's statement, after releasing internal communications, that it was going to discipline employees who wrote them. Needless to say, this type of reaction is absolutely wrong. If Boeing had been listening to its employees, there is a good chance this entire tragic situation never would have happened.

The fallout from the 737 Max situation was catastrophic. Airlines that used the 737 Max had to cancel flights for months, resulting in a loss of revenue and inconvenience for tens of thousands of global travelers. When Boeing announced that it was also suspending production of the aircraft, the decision created cascading effects on hundreds of parts and component manufacturers and suppliers (not to mention the employees of these firms).

Shareholders, of course, also felt the impact. Boeing had more canceled orders than new purchases in 2019. For the first time in at least three decades, Boeing posted negative orders. The company lost 87 orders for commercial airplanes while Airbus, its European competitor, delivered a record 863 new planes.[28] Additionally, the 737 MAX failure forced Boeing to seek $10 billion in loans in order to fix the airplane.[29] Adding debt is not something that shareholders want to hear—nor does anyone else with an interest in the stock market since Boeing is one of the 30 component companies that make up the Dow Jones Industrial Average. All these factors led Treasury Secretary Steven Mnuchin to say that the US economy that was expected to grow at three percent in 2020 could slow to 2.5 percent because of Boeing's problems.[30]

The 737 Max is a classic case study of what *not to do* in a crisis situation. Even more problematic is that Boeing primarily failed from a leadership perspective by:

- Refusing to acknowledge its role in the devastating situation and continuing to stress the safety of the plane when it simply was not true.

- Not listening to its employees who clearly saw problems early on in the plane's development.

- A willingness to sacrifice the long-standing reputation and values of the company for profit.

- A corporate leadership that allowed this type of culture to develop in the first place.

- A cold, impersonal leadership team that issued a hollow statement of sympathies well after the second crash. It wasn't until seven months after the second crash that CEO Dennis Muilenburg decided to meet with families of crash victims. Muilenburg only did so at the urging of Oscar Munoz, then CEO of United Airlines Holdings, who advised him to show more warmth.[31] Munoz had learned about the importance of warmth and compassion after United forcibly removed a ticketed passenger from a flight in 2017. United received justifiable criticism for how it handled that situation.

Getting Ahead of the Problem

One of the most frequently heard solutions to preventing a crisis is to "get ahead of the problem." Some of the issues we have discussed in earlier chapters could have been minimized by the Navy's telling the media about them first rather than being "discovered." For example, Tailhook was the proverbial "train wreck waiting to happen." The Navy had every opportunity—for years—to get out front of the issue and put a stop to it. However, no one had the courage to do so. The Navy could have put an end to the partying, the drinking in the suites, and the other shenanigans and said the event would be strictly a professional symposium. Such a move would have become a one- or two-day story, and Navy leadership would have been lauded for its action. Instead, the Navy had to live with the fallout for years—fallout that brought discredit on an organization that prides itself on a long history of honor, courage, and integrity.

The incident in San Diego when the Navy dropped chaff onto a power station is another example of how *not* to handle a situation. In this case, the Navy simply lied to the public—an entire city, actually—about its role in causing a power outage. Leaders at the time knew exactly what happened that caused the outages and chose to lie about them. The correct action, of course, would have been to say, "Yes. We did it. We're sorry for any damage we may have caused and for the thousands of people we have inconvenienced. It's important that we train in an environment that we may have to fight. But we are sorry that one of our aircraft had a malfunction that led to the dropping of the chaff. We will work with San Diego Gas & Electric to pay for any damages." Instead, we lied and got caught. Were our leaders at the

Naval Air Station arrogant enough to believe that the problem would not be discovered? Naval officers always pride themselves on having integrity. Vice Admiral Easterling, my boss, and I felt betrayed by some of our fellow officers and colleagues.

Some may characterize getting out front of bad news as a communications function. It is—but it really begins as a leadership issue. It takes leaders with courage to say, "Let's get this story out." They are the type of leaders who understand the concept that leaning forward and getting bad news out minimizes its impact.

Let's face reality. If a media member learns about a problem or discovers a newsworthy issue, he or she is going to take credit for "uncovering" the issue. Chances are that the resulting story will be a bit more hard-hitting and/or embarrassing than if an organization gets in front of the issue and announces it first. In the case of the chaff in San Diego, that is exactly what happened. A resident near the power facility told a San Diego media outlet about the chaff found near the power facility—after our denials. The news stories that evening on the 11 p.m. local newscasts were not very pretty. They were embarrassing.

As we have discussed, there are crisis situations that an organization simply cannot plan for—a crash, a fire, or an explosion. Developing a crisis plan, having it in place and practicing it is not only prudent but necessary. It is very clear that Southwest Airlines had a crisis plan and executed it to perfection when the passenger was sucked out of the aircraft. Southwest was able to get out in front of the situation and stay out in front of it.

There are other situations that you can anticipate or plan for—the closure of a plant, the layoff of employees, the elimination of an item from a product line. These situations are much different. Nonetheless, they too require planning.

Then there is the crisis situation that can be prevented from occurring in the first place. This can often be accomplished by providing media access to an organization. We did this at the Naval Academy by providing access to Bancroft Hall where our objective was to showcase leadership being developed. It was that access that influenced reporters from the *Washington Post* and the *Baltimore Sun* not to pursue potentially negative stories about midshipmen passing out from being over-exercised. I equate media access to an insurance policy. You may not know when you are going to have to rely on it but when you do, you will be glad you have it.

Another way to minimize problems is for leadership to listen to their employees. I have had bosses who have repeatedly told their staffs and employees that they do not like surprises—except on their birthday or at Christmas. In essence, they encourage staff members and employees to come forward with bad news. I always found it refreshing to hear a leader say, "That's what I get paid to do—solve problems. Thanks for letting me know. I've got it, and I'll handle it."

On the other hand, I have worked for individuals, or have known individuals, who took the opposite approach and would say things like, "Don't bring me problems. Bring me solutions." Unfortunately, individuals who are aware of problems do not necessarily have a solution to them. The problem or issue is frequently one that can only be resolved by the supervisor or leader. Accordingly, the leader creates an environment that is not conducive to identifying problems, and the issue continues unresolved. It frequently remains unresolved until the media becomes aware of it. Leaders who are prone to "shooting the messenger" exacerbate these situations—leaders who do not take bad news well and lash out at the individual who identifies the problem and brings it forward.

What we have seen at Boeing with the 737 Max issue would lead one to believe that the culture did not encourage employees to come forward when they saw issues and problems. It is clear from some of the employee emails that the culture created at Boeing was one that favored profit over safety. Did the company's culture or leadership encourage employees to come forward with problems? Did leadership have a reputation of "shooting the messenger"?

Engineers identified the design problems with MCAS years before Boeing actually installed the system in the new plane. If the company had taken corrective actions when employees first identified the problems, would the two crashes have occurred? We will probably never know for certain, but the chances are the program would have been approached much more differently.

If one looks at the impact the 737 Max issue has had on Boeing, the word "catastrophic" may be appropriate. Production of the plane stopped, Boeing's orders for new aircraft plummeted, suppliers and their employees have been terribly affected—all leading to the nation's gross domestic product being impacted by a half percentage point.[32]

Democrats on the House of Representatives Transportation & Infrastructure Committee issued a report in March 2020 on Boeing's engineering mistakes and referred to its "culture of concealment."

Those two factors, coupled with a lack of federal safety oversight, led to both the Ethiopian Airlines and Lion Air crashes.

A leadership change that has occurred at Boeing will hopefully resolve the culture questions and create an environment that will allow employees to feel more comfortable and make them feel valued by identifying problems. How the company will recover its reputation is another issue.

Getting in front of problems—or at least minimizing their impact or consequences—comes down to leadership. What is the environment leaders have created? Do they encourage employees to come forward with issues? Are employees rewarded for coming forward? Enlightened leaders are ones who say you cannot solve problems unless you first identify them.

The Takeaway

When faced with a crisis, the public will judge an organization on how quickly and appropriately it handles the situation. The organization can look exceptionally good or exceedingly terrible. Sometimes, an organization can even turn a crisis into an opportunity by showing its preparedness—just like Southwest did.

Is your organization prepared for a crisis? Do you have a plan? Do you practice it? If so, how often do you practice the plan? How realistic is your training?

The basic rules of crisis communications are quite simple.[33] Southwest followed them exceptionally well during its 2018 engine accident; Boeing did not after two 737 Max crashes killed 346 people. Seven rules for crisis communication are as follows:

1. **Respond immediately to a situation**. It is not necessary to wait for all the facts to come in. It is better to provide updates in prepared statements than to let incorrect information and rumors fly around in a void if you are not responding.

2. **Give bad news as soon as possible**. If someone made a mistake, say so and move on. Be honest and direct with the media and the public. Southwest did precisely this in announcing the death of the passenger.

3. **Conduct outreach to all affected parties**. Southwest reached out not only to the family of the deceased passenger but also to

other passengers on the flight. Additionally, it helped to alleviate fears of all customers by outlining the actions it performed to inspect every engine on Southwest planes. Southwest also helped its brand when it allowed the pilot of the damaged aircraft, a female and former Navy pilot, to speak to the media. The public regarded her as a hero for the way she flew the aircraft after the engine failure, despite the death of a passenger. Boeing, on the other hand, did not reach out to passengers for months—possibly on the advice of lawyers who invoked fear into the minds of fellow executives for initiating any form of compassionate outreach. It did so only after an executive from an airline convinced the Boeing CEO to show warmth to family victims.

4. **Have a crisis plan in place that has been fully developed and tested.** Ensure all personnel in the organization are familiar with the elements of the plan and their roles when a crisis happens. Practice the plan and modify it as necessary. Unfortunately, a crisis plan will not serve an organization well if the culture of that organization is grounded in fear of speaking to the public and admitting a mistake. Similarly, a crisis plan will not serve an organization whose culture values profit over safety and honesty and is willing to sacrifice its reputation.

5. **Always avoid the "no comment" comment.** It seems to convey hiding something or worse yet, you are ill-informed, guilty, or both.

6. **Leadership has to be engaged to ensure all guidelines above are followed.** Often, this means making decisions that disagree with other members of the organization. While some may want to "circle the wagons" or take the "head in the sand" approach, a good leader will not allow that to happen.

7. **Create a healthy culture or environment that welcomes the identification of problems and issues.** Actions and plans cannot be made to resolve problems unless the problems or issues are first identified. Boeing's "culture of concealment" discussed in the House's report—*The Boeing 737 Max Aircraft: Costs, Consequences, and Lessons from its Design, Development, and Certification—Preliminary Investigative Findings*—points to the consequences of such a culture.[34]

Notes

1. Fletcher, "A Brief History of the Tylenol Poisonings."
2. Miller and Glick, "The Great Pepsi Panic," 32.
3. Telang and Deshpande, "Keep Calm and Carry on," 371-79.
4. Park, Cha, Kim, and Jeong, "Managing Bad News in Social Media."
5. Ochs, "The Leadership Blind Spots at Wells Fargo."
6. Thesing, "Tesco Drops Silvercrest Foods After Horse Meat Investigation."
7. Blakely, "How Does TESCO Use Social Media?"
8. Hanna, "JetBlue's Valentine's Day Crisis."
9. McCartney, "The Minutes After Disaster Struck," A9.
10. McCartney, A9.
11. McCartney, A9.
12. Victor and Stevens, "United Airlines Passenger is Dragged from an Overbooked Flight."
13. Wikipedia. "Oscar Munoz (Executive)."
14. Slotnick, "Nearly a Year after It Began, the Boeing 737 Max Crisis Still Drags On."
15. Pasztor and Sider, "Chatter at Boeing Undercuts its Defense of MAX Stance," A1.
16. Goldstein, "Boeing Shows 'What Not to Do' in 737 MAX Crisis Communications, Expert Says."
17. Schaper, "737 Max Scandal Cuts Boeing's Once Rock-Solid Image."
18. Schaper, "737 Max Scandal Cuts Boeing's Once Rock-Solid Image."
19. Schaper, "737 Max Scandal Cuts Boeing's Once Rock-Solid Image."
20. Schaper, "737 Max Scandal Cuts Boeing's Once Rock-Solid Image."
21. Pasztor, Tangel, and Mann, "Documents Reveal Warnings at Boeing."
22. Pasztor and Sider, "Chatter at Boeing Undercuts its Defense of MAX Stance," A1.
23. Pasztor and Sider, "Chatter at Boeing Undercuts its Defense of MAX Stance," A1.
24. Pasztor and Sider, "Chatter at Boeing Undercuts its Defense of MAX Stance," A1.
25. Pasztor and Sider, "Chatter at Boeing Undercuts its Defense of MAX Stance," A1.
26. McGregor, "The New CEO of Boeing is Facing a Massive To-do List."
27. Shepardson, Freed, and Hepher, "Boeing Releases Damaging Messages Related to Grounded 737 Max Fleet."
28. Cameron and Katz, "Boeing's Jet Deals Lowest in a Decade."
29. Josephs, "Boeing in Talks to Borrow $10 billion or More as 737 Max Crisis Wears On."
30. Fordham, "America Would Hit 3 Percent Growth without Boeing Problems."
31. Tangel, Sider, and Pasztor, "'We've Been Humbled.'"
32. House, *The Boeing 737 Max Aircraft: Costs, Consequences, and Lessons from its Design, Development, and Certification—Preliminary Investigative Findings*, 3.
33. Obston, "Crisis Public Relations Basic Training."
34. House, *The Boeing 737 Max Aircraft: Costs, Consequences, and Lessons from its Design, Development, and Certification—Preliminary Investigative Findings*, 3.

Chapter 13

The Fundamentals of Good Communications
How to Respond and What to Say

There have been countless workshops, symposia, books, and articles written about how to work with the press, how to handle crises, and what executives need to know when working with the media. Many of these forums primarily focus on what to do when the media arrives at your organization, clamoring for information about a given situation that a business or organization may be facing. Most of the advice provided in these forums, books, and articles has a similar thread and commonality on how to approach these situations. These various how-to approaches are also discussed in the various communication curricula in two-year and four-year college programs.

Over the years, I have compiled my own set of tools and techniques for what it takes to be a reliable communicator and some rules of the road. I collect meaningful articles and tips on leadership and have also amassed a collection of what I think are the essential and significant how-tos for communicators. Some of these articles are quite basic while others are more complex.

McCurry's Five C's

There is, however, one set of principles that is succinct and straightforward. These are defined by Mike McCurry, who "earned his stripes" when he was President Clinton's press secretary. Before he held that position, he served as a spokesman for the US State Department, the Democratic National Committee, two senators, and several presidential candidates.

I know McCurry and can honestly say that I admire both his personal and professional lifestyles. A devotion to religion guides his life. After his 35-year career in national politics and serving several presidential campaigns, McCurry joined the Wesley Seminary as a graduate student. After earning his degree, he became a faculty member who teaches in both the faith and politics curriculum.

I have heard him speak about his role as a communicator on several occasions, and both his delivery and message are quite enjoyable and informative. He can be extremely entertaining while also providing a solid message.

In one speech to the US Navy Public Affairs Association in October 2011, McCurry addressed a broad range of changes affecting our nation and the world, the role of communications, and the failure to communicate. He called his remarks the *Cool Hand Luke* speech and asked his audience to recall the scene in the Paul Newman movie where the jailer reaches over and grabs Newman and says, "What we have here is a failure to communicate."

To help facilitate excellent communication and prevent failure, McCurry focuses on his five C's of communication:

- Credibility
- Candor
- Clarity
- Compassion
- Commitment

Addressing each of these five items, McCurry says credibility means telling the truth. Truth is important.

Candor means we have a hard time dealing with flawed things. Dealing with a mistake or something we have done wrong means having the courage (another "C" that is my contribution to his list) to explain what we have done and what we are going to do to prevent it from happening again.

Clarity means explaining your message clearly and concisely and in language that people will understand. It does not necessarily mean you need to dumb your message down. Just make the information you are providing clear and easy to understand.

Compassion equates to showing respect. So often today, we see both the media and principals involved screaming and shouting over one another. The screaming becomes the focus instead of the issue that should be discussed.

Lastly, McCurry feels there should be a commitment to invest in the communications function. There are certainly some organizations and businesses not committed to a communications function, but I feel most are. Some have made significant investments in this function.

Early in my Navy career, even though the Navy had a cadre of professional communicators, we had a saying in our community: "Last to know, first to go." The significance of that comment was that the PA arm was not always informed about what was going on. Additionally, when budget decisions had to be made, the PA function was left on the proverbial cutting room floor. That is not the case anymore. Although I am biased, the Navy's PA community is probably the most respected of all the military services, and Navy leadership now looks upon PA as a key necessary component of its overall strategy.

I saw this same commitment to a healthy and viable communications function, both internally and externally, at both Lockheed Martin and the US Mint. For example, at Lockheed, there would be a three-day communications symposium each year where all the company's communicators would gather for a series of lectures, workshops, updates, and networking. Putting this on and getting everyone to come to corporate headquarters was expensive, but it reflected the strong commitment and importance Lockheed placed on communications. The president and CEO, CFO, and other critical senior leaders always provided presentations and updates.

Principles for Working with the Media

One speaker who addressed one of our annual gatherings was Ari Fleischer, a former press secretary to Pres. George W. Bush. During his lecture, Fleischer presented his principles for working with the media. I provide them below, along with some personal embellishments and additives:

1. **Always tell the truth and ensure your bosses do.** This seems like a basic tenet; however, the Navy could have prevented suffering from the consequences of Tailhook '91 if leadership had commanded that everyone "come clean" and cooperate with investigators. The Navy did not do itself any favors by conducting sloppy in-house investigations into the whole matter. The antics and criminal activity at Tailhook '91 should have been rooted out years before the nightmare. Countless people were warning about it for years, but leaders were afraid to "break china." Sometimes china has to be broken and leadership must have the courage to do it. As a result, the train wreck was inevitable. To this day, the word Tailhook is still used when referring to sexual harassment in the military.

2. **Communicators should look upon themselves as counselors for their boss.** As a communicator, you must tell your boss what he or she needs to hear, not always what they want to hear. If you are the boss, you must listen to your advisors and not

hold it against them for speaking up. This is not the easiest thing to do. As the messenger, you are always concerned about possible repercussions. Also, it takes time to develop a comfort level that enables you to approach the boss and say that the chosen direction is the wrong one. Again, it comes down to having the courage to do the right thing for the benefit of the organization.

3. **Do your homework and attend the right meetings.** If you find yourself on the outside looking in and not aware of what is happening because you are not in the right meetings, you can solve this problem in a couple of ways. One method is to go to the various department heads (colleagues) and tell them you heard about meeting A, B, or C and that you feel you should have been there because you could have learned something from that session. You can also go to your boss and state that you would like to be considered for inclusion in some of the meetings he or she leads. You could convey that being included will provide you more depth and insight into various issues. I have done this with many of my bosses, and the typical response from leadership has been "Of course" or "Absolutely—you're right and I'll be more aware of that in the future and be sure to include you." Sometimes, the person who has called a meeting simply has not thought about the possible communications impact of an issue.

4. **Do not limit your facetime with colleagues to staff meetings. Be visible.** Get out of your office and visit the CFO, the marketing head, the legal department, the human resources chief, or any number of other executives in your organization. If you are a junior communications staff member, seek out an equivalent staff member in each department. Sit down with them and see what is going on in their departments. What are their significant issues and challenges? Tell them what you are working on and what your big issues are. If you rely on getting the "story behind the story" or what is really going on in the organization from the weekly staff or department head meeting, you will be sadly disappointed. By roaming the organization, you can often learn of problems or issues before they happen. One of the worst things that can happen to a communicator is having a reporter tell you what is going on in your organization.

5. **The message, the message, the message.** When preparing for a media interview, or when merely talking to a reporter, write your messaging and talking points down. Write the headline or the one takeaway message you would like to come out of the interview—and keep coming back to it in your interview. When preparing your boss for a media session, provide him or her the same guidance and counsel. If an interview is conducted over the phone, have your messages written and spread out over your desk as you speak.

6. **Think like a reporter.** When preparing for a media interview, think like a reporter. What are the tough questions he or she will ask? Some bosses will negatively react when you bring up this type of questioning in advance. I call them "dirty questions." Many bosses will say, "That's not a fair question. Tell the reporter not to ask it," or "I'll be damned if I'm going to answer that question." However, more often than not, it *is* a fair question and your boss should be ready to answer it with a graceful, truthful, and direct answer. To go into an interview "loaded for bear" is not in your boss's or organization's best interest.

7. **Develop relationships with reporters.** I cannot overemphasize the importance of building relationships with reporters. They do not have to be your new best friends, but you need them as much as they need you—especially when it comes to a crisis. At that point, it is too late to begin developing a relationship with the reporter. You begin to develop relationships with reporters by talking with them—in person or on the phone—not via email, texting, or on social media. As you cultivate these professional relationships, trust will develop. Trust is the foundation of working with the media and it is evident when you start having off-the-record or background conversations with a reporter. Often, a PR person will brag about the number of stories he or she has placed. My belief is the real value of a professional communicator is the number of stories that he or she has killed or delayed because of a relationship that exists with a specific reporter. You do this by offering them a side of the story that they are unaware of when they contact you. Through this education and discussion, a reporter will delay filing a story or realize there is not a story to follow.

Sometimes a story can even be delayed and given a more vibrant and deeper context. Again, this results from a communicator's relationship with a media representative—reporter, producer, or editor. For example, many reporters will sit on a story for an additional day or two if they know a "subject matter expert" will be made available to them and provide them with in-depth and more accurate information. Again, this will not always happen unless there is a preexisting positive relationship. A new wrinkle in working with the media is the propensity for younger communicators to rely on digital and social media to communicate with reporters. I think there is a time and a place to use electronic communications when working with the press, but I still favor communicating the "good old-fashioned way"—voice to voice or in-person. I do not prefer to even to leave a voice mail, unless it is to say you have something for the reporter and to call you.

When I first started at Lockheed Martin, email was still a relatively new communications tool and its use was still being refined. Whenever I saw an inaccurate fact or policy in a story, I would ask one of my staff members to contact the reporter and to be sure the reporter knew there was an error in a story he or she had written. Some of the errors were minor; however, some were a bit more significant. Late in the day or the next day, I would ask my team member if they called reporter X or Y and corrected the inaccuracy in the story.

Often the response would be, "Yes. I did. I sent him an email with the correct information."

"No," I would say. "Please call the reporter, tell him or her about the error." Any reporter worth their salt wants to know if a mistake was made directly. This is also an excellent opportunity to pick up the phone and call that reporter to convey what is incorrect. It is a wonderful opportunity for you to get to know the reporter and establish a relationship. Listen to the inflection in the reporter's voice. Perhaps you can learn what else the reporter is working on—or even learn what a competitor is working on. I call this intelligence and it is good to have in your back pocket.

When I departed Lockheed, one of the most gratifying things my staff said to me was how important it was to talk to reporters and develop relationships with them versus relying strictly on email communication. I felt I had succeeded in teaching my staff something about working with the press. I think they learned that cultivating these relationships was like "money in the bank."

8. Respond immediately to adverse situations. Some leaders believe that problems or issues will disappear simply by not addressing them. While the media wait for answers about why a hazardous material team was seen at one of your company's plants, rumors begin. Employees who are not "in the know" begin to talk among themselves and say they heard this, that, or some other thing. Before you know it, employees are posting information on social media and the media are viewing it. Therefore, you have created this misleading situation by not communicating inside and outside your organization as quickly as possible. Unfortunately, the company has done this to itself and created another problem it now has to face. In addition to the incident, accident, or whatever the problem was, the company now is the subject in the media of how poorly it handled the matter.

In addition to being prepared to handle emergencies or crises from an external perspective, you cannot overlook your employees. Whatever statement you provide to the media, you should provide to your employees. With digital communications and social media being prevalent, employees are easily informed, so there is every reason to convey the message.

As a footnote to that, though, in many factory environments there are still employees who do *not* have access to computers. For example, at the US Mint, employees who worked on the production floor producing coins did not have ready access to a computer. They clocked in at the beginning of the day and clocked out when their shift was over. Supervisors, managers, and the communications team must not forget communicating to these employees—even if it means providing them a hard copy statement, providing them a hard copy of a digital newsletter, or simply communicating with them verbally as they complete their shift.

9. Just say "No" to "No comment." Responding to any situation with a "no comment" statement is tantamount to saying, "I know we did something wrong, but we're just not going to admit it." Instead, there are a myriad of ways to respond to a tough situation. Here are some examples:

- Because the matter is under investigation, it would be inappropriate to offer details at this time;
- Because of pending litigation, it would be inappropriate to comment; or
- We are interviewing several individuals who may have seen the accident. As we speak with them, we will be able to provide you some information.

There are numerous ways to talk around an issue until an organization is prepared to be more forthcoming. However, responding with a "no comment" is *not* one of them. For many leaders, offering a "no comment" response shows a bit of machismo—a sort of "I'll show you who the boss is." "No comment" also throws down a gauntlet and sends an uncooperative signal to the media. It is not the type of signal that an organization or its leadership wants to send. Unfortunately, lawyers portrayed in television shows perpetuate this when they duck questions from reporters.

However, there are points in a crisis when updates should be provided to the media. During the Southwest Airlines engine failure in 2018, Southwest did so. As information became available and could be confirmed, Southwest provided updates electronically. The advantage of providing timely, reliable updates is that it precludes both the origination and spread of rumors. Often, however, despite your best efforts, some crises become so chaotic that you cannot disseminate updated information because you don't yet have all the information.

Public Affairs in the Government Sector

Being a communicator in the federal government is not any different than being one in the private sector when it comes to operational philosophy. The only real difference is that being a communicator in the private sector, especially in the corporate world, mandates an understanding of business and finance. When I transitioned from the Navy to Lockheed Martin, I was very intimidated and concerned about my lack of finance knowledge. However, I was blessed to have worked with professional staff from the finance and legal teams at Lockheed. They were patient when explaining SEC filings, requirements for reporting quarterly earnings, explaining the importance of adhering to "quiet periods" when a company is prohibited from making public statements before the close of a quarter, how we work with Wall Street analysts, and the necessary communications steps involving a merger or acquisition.

There were several constants in both sectors, including responding truthfully and quickly to the media and being transparent in our dealings with them. Besides, just as the government sector has shareholders, Lockheed Martin has shareholders to whom they are responsible.

When I was the chief of information for the Navy—I served as the Navy's chief PA officer—I was extremely fortunate to have a positive relationship with the Assistant Secretary of Defense for Public Affairs, Mr. Ken Bacon. Bacon was a former reporter and editor for the *Wall Street Journal* and tapped to serve as the DOD spokesman for Defense Secretary William Perry and afterwards for William Cohen—both defense secretaries serving in the Clinton administration.

Bacon was a good leader and regularly gathered all the service information chiefs—my counterparts in the Army, Air Force, Marine Corps, and Coast Guard. During our meetings, Bacon provided insight on events occurring in the DOD and kept us apprised of unfamiliar political issues. Because of our meetings, the service information chiefs shared information and sought each other's counsel on sensitive issues. As a result, the service information chiefs had a great relationship with one another because of Bacon's leadership and our desire to be team players.

During Bacon's tenure as the DOD spokesman, he developed a policy regarding the promulgation of information to the public, Congress, and the media. The policy, approved and signed by Secretary of Defense Cohen, was called the *Principles of Information*. The policy lives on today, but more importantly, I hope it is enforced. The *Principles of Information* read as follows:

> It is the policy of the Department of Defense to make available timely and accurate information so that the public, Congress, and the news media may assess and understand the facts about national security and defense strategy.

Requests for information from organizations and private citizens will be answered in a timely manner. In carrying out the policy, the following principles of information will apply:

Information will be made fully and readily available, consistent with statutory requirements, unless its release is precluded by current and valid security classification. The provisions of the Freedom of Information Act will be supported in both letter and spirit.

A free flow of information will be made available, without censorship or propaganda, to the men and women of the Armed Services and their dependents.

Information will not be classified or otherwise withheld to protect the government from criticism or embarrassment.

Information will be withheld only when disclosure would adversely affect national security or threaten the safety or privacy of the men and women of the Armed Forces.

The Department's obligation to provide the public with information on its major programs may require detailed public affairs planning and coordination within the Department and with other government agencies. The sole purpose of such activity is to expedite the flow of information to the public; propaganda has no place in Department of Defense public affairs programs.

The Assistant Secretary of Defense for Public Affairs has the primary responsibility for carrying out this commitment.[1]

In 2000, then Secretary of Defense Donald Rumsfeld reissued and signed these same principles. They are as pertinent now as they were in 1997 when Bacon developed them. *All* government leaders and communicators should be reminded of these principles because they go to the heart of what it means to be a public servant. Those in government have a responsibility to those they serve, and the *Principles of Information* represent the framework for public service.

Notes

1. Department of Defense, *Principles of Information.*

Chapter 14

Final Tips

When You Meet the Media

The Navy and its cadre of PA professionals always pride themselves on their reputation. We feel we are better trained and equipped to deal with the media than the other services and government agencies. This was reinforced when reporters who were part of the Pentagon press corps said we were the best military service when it came to working with the media.

We prided ourselves on our media-training program. We put a vibrant, robust, and aggressive program together and offered that training to senior officials—both military and civilian—who had the potential to engage the media. During the training, we focused on several things that we felt were critical to a successful interface with the media.

First of all, like Mike McCurry's five "C's," we offered trainees our own "C's"—but in this case, four of them:

- Commercials: Decide two or three communication points you want to get across. Anticipate questions and how you can weave commercials into your responses.

- Control: Be positive in your attitude. Do not be passive. Answer questions with your commercial in mind. Be prepared. Be concise.

- Cosmetics: Look your best.

- Commandment: Thou shalt not lie.

We also offered some basic interview tips to our trainees:

- Believe that the reporter represents the public and the public has the right and need to know.

- Know why you were asked for the interview. Know your audience. Arrive early.

- Do your homework. Be aware of what is happening, not only in your shop but also in your entire organization. For example, should you be aware of something happening at your headquarters?

- Question your position beforehand—play devil's advocate with yourself. An even better approach is to ensure staff members role-play as devil's advocates as you prepare for the interview. A common characterization for these sessions is a "murder board."[1]

- Establish ground rules with the reporter/producer, such as length of the interview, subjects to be discussed, and how you will be identified (by name, rank, and position or as an "official," and so forth).

- Also, ask, "Is the interview on-the-record? Background? Deep background?" There are apparent differences among these, and interviewees need to be aware of them. "On-the-record" means everything you say can be attributed to you. Going on "background" means you are providing the reporter information that opens up the reporter's understanding of an issue and offers a bit more perspective. This information can be used but you need to agree with the reporter about how it will be attributed. For example, you could ask the reporter to cite "an individual familiar with the situation," "a knowledgeable source," and so on. "Deep background," on the other hand, means you are providing information to the reporter that also provides a better perspective; however, this information cannot be used. Be sure to understand that "background" and "deep background" frequently have different meanings for different reporters. Therefore, you must discuss these differences in meaning with the media representative who is interviewing you to ensure your understanding of the terms is the same.

- As a matter of note, be cautious when using off-the-record comments. Off-the-record does not mean a reporter cannot use the information you provide. It simply means they can take that information and get a response from another source. Stated another way, do not say anything you do not want to see or hear the next day from another reporter.

A good example of why off-the-record comments should be used cautiously is the case of Madeleine Westerhout, the long-time personal secretary to Pres. Donald Trump and director of Oval Office operations at the White House. Westerhout was having an off-the-record dinner with reporters one evening when she made some comments about the Trump family.[2] The comments were reported and Westerhout was dismissed from her job by the president.[3]

- Be confident. You are the subject expert, while most reporters are generalists.
- Establish a professional rapport with the reporter. Be cooperative.
- Use short responses. Make your point clear and do not say anything extra. Do not "feed" the microphone. One tactic of many reporters is to not respond to an interviewee's statement, and instead to pause and say nothing. That long awkward pause can cause an interviewee to feel as if they *must* say something. Again, make your point and conclude the interview.
- Put your conclusion first, and then expand.
- Speak the public's language—do not use jargon or acronyms in your responses—especially when it comes to technical or military topics.
- If you do not know something, say so. Do not "snow" the reporter. Offer to find answers to questions that you cannot answer and indicate you or your PA officer will follow up on the question.
- Do not use "No comment." State why you cannot answer—"That question is one of the things that is part of our ongoing investigation," or "That is a matter that is not under my purview, and therefore, it would be inappropriate for me to speak on that subject."
- Do not accept a reporter's facts or any misinformation at face value. Verify the information, and if needed, correct the record.
- Avoid responding to hypothetical questions.
- Keep your composure under fire. Do not argue and do not repeat negative words or inaccurate information expressed in the question.
- Keep personal opinions to a minimum.
- Be familiar with current headlines in the news. Do not be taken by surprise as you may be asked about something that just broke in the news. Before doing an interview, a quick look at a few online news sites to get caught up is a good idea.
- Listen carefully to questions that are being asked.

Notes

1. The term murder board is not nearly as bad as it sounds. The term actually has its roots in the military, but it is also used effectively in the academic, communications, government, legal, and business worlds to prepare leaders for interviews, congressional hearings, and court testimony. It's a great way for leaders to be prepared for the tough questions they may receive in any of the above venues. See Audacia Strategies, "Murder Board: It's Not as Bad as It Sounds. How to Use Criticism to Prepare Your Team."

2. Budryk, "Madeline Westerhout to Release White House Memoir in August."

3. Westerhout, *Off the Record: Picking Up the Pieces after Losing My Dream Job at the White House.*

Postscript

As this book went to print, our nation was suffering from a global pandemic named COVID-19. The pandemic illustrated the importance of—and demand for—honest, open, and forthright communications. Similarly, the pandemic demonstrated the importance of credible leaders at the federal, state, and local levels who were willing to tell the citizenry what they needed to hear as we all coped with the pandemic. As the world works at press time to find a vaccine that will fight the silent enemy called "Coronavirus 19," there will be countless examples of communications and leadership—both good and bad—that perhaps we can document in another publication.

Abbreviations

CEO	chief executive officer
CFO	chief financial officer
CNO	chief of naval operations
FDA	Food and Drug Administration
GAO	Government Accountability Office
IG	inspector general
JSF	Joint Strike Fighter
NCIS	Naval Criminal Investigative Service
NIS	Naval Investigative Service
OCS	Officer Candidate School
OIG	Office of Inspector General
OMB	Office of Management and Budget
PA	public affairs
PR	public relations
ROTC	Reserve Officer Training Corps
SDG&E	San Diego Gas and Electric
SEAL	Sea-Air-Land
SEC	Securities and Exchange Commission
USS	United States Ship

Bibliography

13 Former White House Press Secretaries, Foreign Service, and Military Officials. "Why America Needs to Hear from Its Government." CNN, 11 January 2020. https://www.cnn.com/.

"America the Beautiful Quarters." CoinNews Media. 17 February 2010. GroupAmericaBeautifulQuarters.com. https://web.archive.org/.

Antonelli, Kris, "Naval Academy Tests for Drugs Action Taken in Wake of Arrest of Two Midshipmen." *Baltimore Sun*, 17 October 1995. https://www.baltimoresun.com/.

Audacia Strategies. "Murder Board: It's Not as Bad as It Sounds. How to Use Criticism to Prepare Your Team." 30 April 2018. https://audaciastrategies.com/.

Barringer, Felicity. "Harassment of Woman Shakes Naval Academy." *New York Times*, 20 May 1990. https://www.nytimes.com/.

Battleship Iowa Museum. "Learn the History." Pacific Battleship Center. https://www.pacificbattleship.com.

Beck, Robert L. "Guest Column: Author Recounts How Navy Has Changed Since Tailhook in 1991." *Florida Times Union,* 15 September 2016. https://www.jacksonville.com.

——. "Guest Column: Tailhook Started Huge Changes." *Capital Gazette*, 3 September 2016. https://www.capitalgazette.com.

——. *Inside The Tailhook Scandal: A Naval Aviator's Story.* Meadville, PA: Fulton Books, 2016.

Blakely, Alex. "How Does TESCO Use Social Media?" Giraffe Social Media, 11 October 2013. https://www.giraffesocialmedia.co.uk/.

Blumenthal, Dannielle. "The Difference between Public Affairs and Public Relations." *Government Executive*, 17 September 2015. https://www.govexec.com.

Boomer, Walter. "Stop Whining." *Proceedings*, no. 123/7/1,133 (July 1997): 2. https://www.usni.org/.

Budryk, Zack. "Madeleine Westerhout to Release White House Memoir in August." *The Hill,* 16 March 2020. https://thehill.com/.

Cameron, Doug, and Benjamin Katz. "Boeing's Jet Deals Lowest in a Decade." *Wall Street Journal,* 15 January 2020. https://www.morningstar.com/.

Cardona, Claire. "What You Need to Know About the Teenage Love Triangle that Sent the Texas 'Cadet Killers' to Prison 20 Years Ago." *Dallas Morning News*, 24 July 2018. https://www.dallasnews.com/.

Department of Defense. *Principles of Information.* Enclosure (2) to Department of Defense Directive 5122.5. Washington, DC: 27 September 2000. https://www.defense.gov/Resources/Principles -of-Information/.

——. *Tailhook 91, Part 1, Review of the Navy Investigations.* Arlington, VA: Office of Inspector General, September 1992. http://ncisa history.org.

——. *Tailhook 91, Part 2, Events of the 35th Annual Tailhook Symposium.* Arlington, VA: Office of Inspector General, April 1993. https://apps.dtic.mil.

Farley, Robert. "How the Soviet Union and China Almost Started World War III." *National Interest,* 9 February 2016. https://national interest.org.

Fletcher, Dan. "A Brief History of the Tylenol Poisonings." *Time,* 2009. http://content.time.com/.

Fordham, Evie. "America Would Hit 3 Percent Growth without Boeing Problems." *Fox Business,* 12 January 2020. https://www.foxbusi ness.com/.

Freed, David. "Navy Denies Being Cause of Blackout: SDG&E Seeks Reasons Behind Power Outage to See Who'll Pay for Damages," *Los Angeles Times,* 12 January 1985. http://articles.latimes.com/.

Goldstein, Michael. "Boeing Shows 'What Not to Do' in 737 MAX Crisis Communications, Expert Says." *Forbes,* 18 March 2019. https://www.forbes.com/.

Grove, Thomas. "Russia and China Plan Joint War Games." *Wall Street Journal,* 29 August 2018.

Hanna, Julia. "JetBlue's Valentine's Day Crisis." *Working Knowledge.* Harvard Business School, 31 March 2008. https://hbswk.hbs.edu/.

Healy, Melissa. "Pentagon Blasts Tailhook Probe, Two Admirals Resign." *Los Angeles Times,* 25 September 1992. http://tech.mit.edu.

Healy, Melissa, and Nora Zamichow. "Navy Suspends Operations to Review Safety." *Los Angeles Times,* 15 November 1989. https:// www.latimes.com.

History.com Editors. "Gorbachev Resigns as President of the USSR." *History,* 13 November 2009. https://www.history.com.

"Hot Springs National Park Quarter." *America the Beautiful Quarters.* CoinNews Media. 17 February 2010. GroupAmericaBeautiful-Quarters.com. https://web.archive.org/.

House. *The Boeing 737 Max Aircraft: Costs, Consequences, and Lessons from its Design, Development, and Certification—Preliminary*

Investigative Findings. House Committee on Transportation & Infrastructure. 116th Cong., 1st sess., 2020. https://transportation .house.gov/.

Hurst, John, and Melissa Healy. "Navy Planes Bomb Desert Campground." *Los Angeles Times*, 14 November 1989. https://www.latimes .com.

Jones, Frank L. *A Hollow Army Reappraised: President Carter, Defense Budgets, and the Politics of Military Readiness.* Army War College: Strategic Studies Institute, Carlisle, PA, 2012. https://apps.dtic .mil/dtic/tr/fulltext/u2/a566298.pdf.

Josephs, Leslie. "Boeing in Talks to Borrow $10 billion or More as 737 Max Crisis Wears On," CNBC, 20 January 2020. https://cnbc.com/.

Larson, Eric V., David T. Orletsky, and Kristin J. Leuschner. *Defense Planning in a Decade of Change: Lessons from the Base Force, Bottom-Up Review, and Quadrennial Defense Review.* Santa Monica, CA: RAND Corporation, Project AIR FORCE, 2001. https://www .rand.org.

Lazer, David M. J., Matthew A. Baum, Yochai Benkler, Adam J. Berinsky, Kelly M. Greenhill, Filippo Menczer, Miriam J. Metzger et al. "The Science of Fake News." *Science* 359, no. 6380 (2018): 1094–96.

Lessing, Doris. *African Laughter.* New York: HarperCollins, 1992.

Lewis, Neil A. "Tailhook Affair Brings Censure of 3 Admirals." *New York Times*, 15 October 1993.

Lukaszewski, James E. "Strengthening Corporate Trust in Times of Crisis (Part 1)." *Ethikos and Corporate Conduct Quarterly* 22, no. 6 (May/June 2009): 11–15. https://assets.corporatecompliance.org.

McCartney, Scott. "The Minutes After Disaster Struck." *Wall Street Journal*, 25 April 2017.

McGregor, Jenna. "The New CEO of Boeing Is Facing a Massive To-do List." *Washington Post*, 12 January 2020.

McMichael, William H. *The Mother of All Hooks.* New Brunswick, NJ: Transaction Publishers, 1997.

"Midshipman Leaves Naval Academy after Classmates Tie Her to Urinal." AP News, 13 May 1990. https://apnews.com/.

Miller, Annetta, and Daniel Glick. "The Great Pepsi Panic." *Newsweek* 121, no. 26 (1993): 32.

Obston, Andrea. "Crisis Public Relations Basic Training for Executives: What to Do When Reporters Are Banging On Your Door." *Tips and Tactics* 38, no. 10. Supplement of *PR Reporter*, 14 August 2000.

Ochs, Susan M. "The Leadership Blind Spots at Wells Fargo." *Harvard Business Review* 10 (2016). https://hbr.org/.

Park, Jaram, Meeyoung Cha, Hoh Kim, and Jaeseung Jeong. "Managing Bad News in Social Media: A Case Study on Domino's Pizza Crisis." In *Sixth International AAAI Conference on Weblogs and Social Media*. 2012. https://www.aaai.org/.

Partnership for Public Service. "Ten Years of the Best Places to Work in the Federal Government Rankings: How Six Federal Agencies Improved Employee Satisfaction and Commitment." September 2013. https://www.opm.gov/.

Pasztor, Andy, and Alison Sider. "Chatter at Boeing Undercuts Its Defense Stance." *Wall Street Journal*, 11–12 January 2020. https://www.wsj.com/.

Pasztor, Andy, Andrew Tangel, and Ted Mann. "Documents Reveal Warnings at Boeing," *Wall Street Journal*, 31 October 2019. https://www.advfn.com/.

Schaper, David. "737 Max Scandal Cuts Boeing's Once Rock-Solid Image," *NPR Morning Edition*, 26 November 2019. https://www.npr.org/.

Shepardson, David, Jamie Freed, and Tim Hepher. "Boeing Releases Damaging Messages Related to Grounded 737 Max Fleet," Reuters, 9 January 2020.

Schmitt, Eric, "An Inquiry Finds 125 Cheated on a Naval Academy Exam." *New York Times*, 13 January 1994. https://www.nytimes.com/.

Shellenberger, Sue. "The Best Bosses Are Humble Bosses." *Wall Street Journal*, 10 October 2018.

Shen, Fern. "Probe Finds Extensive Coverup of Cheating at Naval Academy." *Washington Post*, 25 January 1994.

Slotnick, David. "Nearly a Year after It Began, the Boeing 737 Max Crisis Still Drags On. Here's the Complete History of the Plane That's Been Grounded since 2 Crashes Killed 346 People 5 Months Apart." *Business Insider*, 5 March 2020. https://www.businessinsider.com/.

Spears, Sally. *Call Sign Revlon: The Life and Death of Navy Fighter Pilot Kara Hultgreen*. Annapolis, MD: Naval Institute Press, 1998.

Sullam, Brian. "Some at Academy Did Right Thing in Murder." *New York Daily News*, 22 September 1996. https://www.nydailynews.com/.

"Tailhook '91." PBS *Frontline*. https://www.pbs.org.

Tangel, Andrew, Alison Sider, and Andy Pasztor. "'We've Been Humbled': Boeing's CEO Struggles to Contain 737 Max Crisis." *Wall Street Journal*, 23 December 2019.

Telang, A., and A. Deshpande. "Keep Calm and Carry on: A Crisis Communication Study of Cadbury and McDonalds." *Management & Marketing. Challenges for the Knowledge Society* 11, no. 1 (2016): 371–79. https://www.degruyter.com/.

"The Combined Joint Task Forces Concept." NATO. 1999. https://www.nato.int/.

The Dollar Coin Alliance, "Facts About the Dollar Coin." http://www.dollarcoinalliance.org/.

Thesing, Gabi. "Tesco Drops Silvercrest Foods After Horse Meat Investigation." *Bloomberg News*, 30 January 2013.

The White House. "Campaign to Cut Waste." https://obamawhitehouse.archives.gov/.

To Thomas Jefferson from John Adams, 25 August 1787," Founders Online, National Archives. https://founders.archives.gov/.

Tyler, Patrick E. "Life on Carrier Shows Danger Part of the Job." *Daily Press*, 3 January 1990. http://www.dailypress.com.

Vanden Brook, Tom. "Bad Santa: Pentagon Releases Report on Sexual Harassment at Navy's Boozy Christmas Bash." *USA Today*, 12 October 2018. https://www.usatoday.com.

Venable, Heather P. *How the Few Became the Proud: Crafting the Marine Corps Mystique, 1874–1918 (Transforming War)*. Annapolis, MD: Naval Institute Press, 2019.

Victor, Daniel, and Matt Stevens. "United Airlines Passenger Is Dragged from an Overbooked Flight." *New York Times*, 10 April 2017. https://www.nytimes.com/.

Vistica, Gregory L. *Fall from Glory: The Men Who Sank the U.S. Navy*. New York: Simon and Schuster, 1997.

——. "On the Frontier of Soviet-Chinese Relations. Once Tense Border of U.S.S.R., China Now Booming Trade Zone." *San Diego Union*, 27 September 1990.

Waddle, Ryan D. *Selling Sea Power: Public Relations and the U.S. Navy, 1917–1941*. Norman, OK: University of Oklahoma Press, 2019

Webb, James. "The Navy Adrift." *Washington Post*, Opinion Section, 28 April 1996.

Weintraub, Daniel M. "Navy to Pay SDG&E; for Chaff Damage." *Los Angeles Times*, 30 July 1985. http://articles.latimes.com/.

Westerhout, Madeline. Forthcoming. *Off the Record: Picking Up the Pieces after Losing My Dream Job at the White House.* New York: Hachette Book Group, 2020.

Wikipedia. "E Ticket." Last modified 4 September 2019. https://en.wikipedia.org/.

_____. "Loonie." Last modified 29 March 2020. https://en.m.wikipedia.org/.

_____. "Oscar Munoz (Executive)." Last modified 15 January 2020. https://en.wikipedia.org/.

_____. "Sacagawea Dollar." Last modified 11 March 2020. https://en.wikipedia.org/.

_____. "Titan Corporation." Last modified 10 September 2019. https://en.wikipedia.org/.

Zimmerman, Stan. "The Battle of the Lasting Impression." *Proceedings* 123, no. 5, 1,131 (May 1997): 44–47. https://www.usni.org/.

Index